FLYING MACHINE

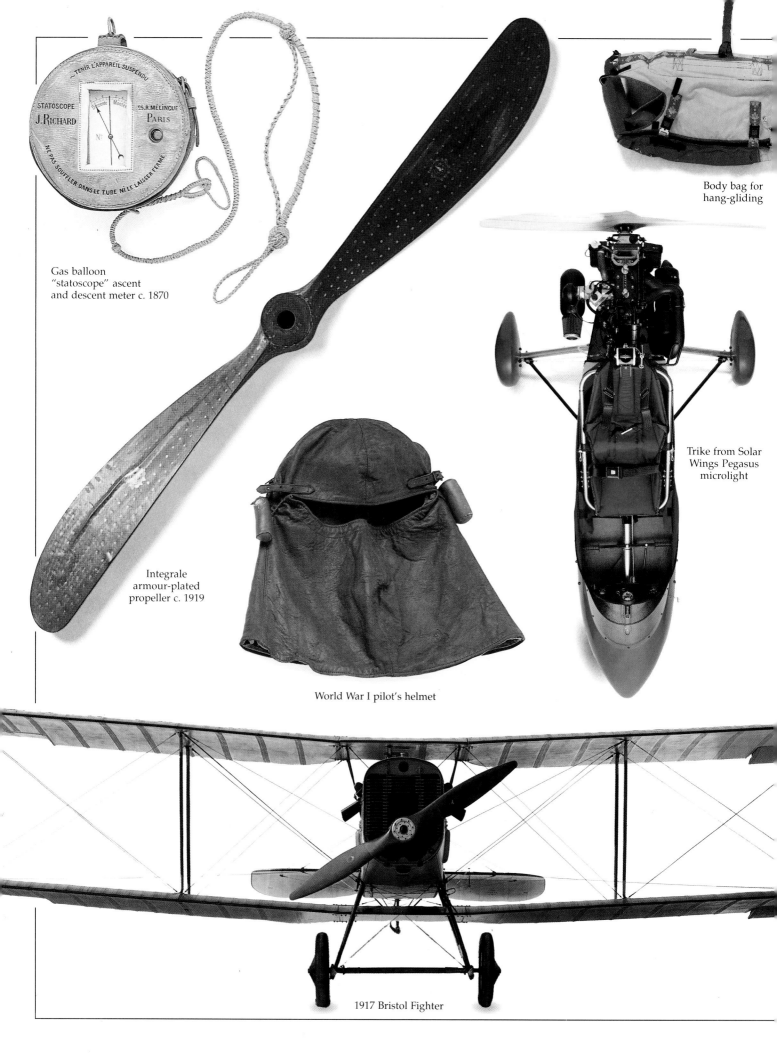

Gas balloon
"statoscope" ascent
and descent meter c. 1870

STATOSCOPE
J. RICHARD
PARIS
25, R. MELINGUE

TENIR L'APPAREIL SUSPENDU

NE PAS SOUFFLER DANS LE TUBE NI LE LAISSER FERMÉ

Body bag for
hang-gliding

Trike from Solar
Wings Pegasus
microlight

Integrale
armour-plated
propeller c. 1919

World War I pilot's helmet

1917 Bristol Fighter

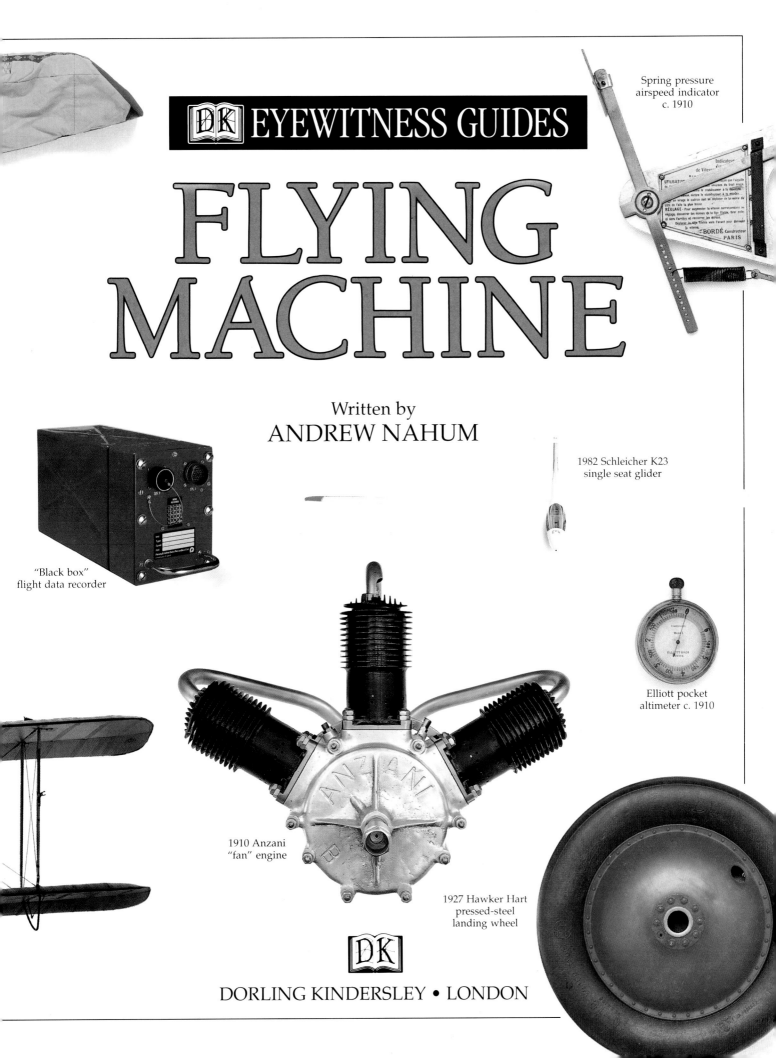

DK EYEWITNESS GUIDES

FLYING MACHINE

Written by
ANDREW NAHUM

Spring pressure
airspeed indicator
c. 1910

1982 Schleicher K23
single seat glider

"Black box"
flight data recorder

Elliott pocket
altimeter c. 1910

1910 Anzani
"fan" engine

1927 Hawker Hart
pressed-steel
landing wheel

DORLING KINDERSLEY • LONDON

Undercarriage from
1909 Deperdussin

Front fan from
Rolls-Royce Tay
turbofan engine

1909 Paragon
experimental
propeller blade

DK

A DORLING KINDERSLEY BOOK

Project editor John Farndon
Art editor Mark Richards
Managing editor Sophie Mitchell
Senior art editor Julia Harris
Editorial director Sue Unstead
Art director Anne-Marie Bulat
Special photography Dave King,
Peter Chadwick, and Mike Dunning

Mach meter c. 1960

This Eyewitness ® Guide has been
conceived by Dorling Kindersley Limited
and Editions Gallimard

First published in Great Britain in 1990
by Dorling Kindersley Limited,
9 Henrietta Street, London, WC2E 8PS

8 10 9

Copyright © 1990 Dorling Kindersley Limited, London

Visit us on the World Wide Web at
http://www.dk.com

Engine
parts from
Henson and
Stringfellow's
Aerial Steam
Carriage
of 1845

British Library Cataloguing in Publication Data
Nahum, Andrew
  Flying machine.
  1. Aircraft
  I. Title II. Series
  629.133

ISBN 0-86318-413-8

Colour reproduction by Colourscan, Singapore
Typeset by Windsorgraphics, Ringwood, Hampshire
Printed in China by Toppan Printing Co., (Shenzhen) Ltd.

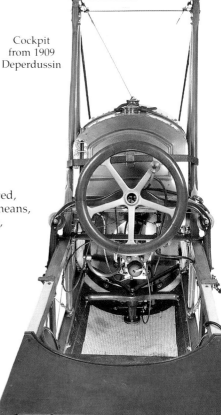

Cockpit
from 1909
Deperdussin

Contents

World War I goggles
and map case

Flying like a bird

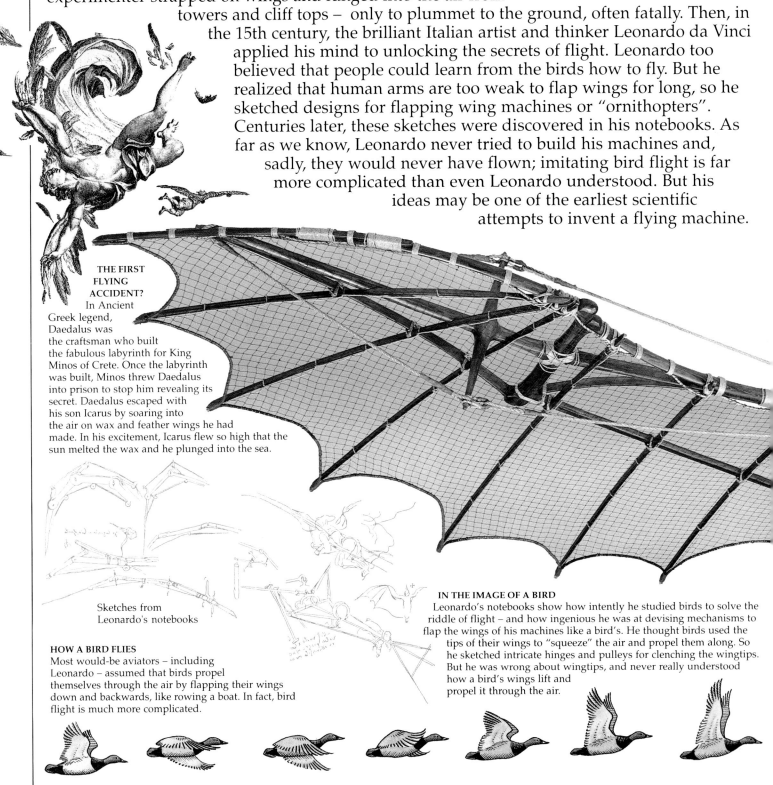

Sɪɴᴄᴇ ᴛʜᴇ ᴅᴀʏꜱ of the mythical birdman Daedalus in ancient Greece, people have longed to fly like the birds. For centuries, some believed that if they could mimic the birds and their flapping wings, they too would be able to fly. In the Middle Ages in Europe, many a reckless experimenter strapped on wings and lunged into the air from towers and cliff tops – only to plummet to the ground, often fatally. Then, in the 15th century, the brilliant Italian artist and thinker Leonardo da Vinci applied his mind to unlocking the secrets of flight. Leonardo too believed that people could learn from the birds how to fly. But he realized that human arms are too weak to flap wings for long, so he sketched designs for flapping wing machines or "ornithopters". Centuries later, these sketches were discovered in his notebooks. As far as we know, Leonardo never tried to build his machines and, sadly, they would never have flown; imitating bird flight is far more complicated than even Leonardo understood. But his ideas may be one of the earliest scientific attempts to invent a flying machine.

FLYING DUCKS
In 1678, a French locksmith called Besnier tried to fly with wings that worked like the webbed feet of a duck. He was lucky to land alive.

THE FIRST FLYING ACCIDENT?
In Ancient Greek legend, Daedalus was the craftsman who built the fabulous labyrinth for King Minos of Crete. Once the labyrinth was built, Minos threw Daedalus into prison to stop him revealing its secret. Daedalus escaped with his son Icarus by soaring into the air on wax and feather wings he had made. In his excitement, Icarus flew so high that the sun melted the wax and he plunged into the sea.

Sketches from Leonardo's notebooks

HOW A BIRD FLIES
Most would-be aviators – including Leonardo – assumed that birds propel themselves through the air by flapping their wings down and backwards, like rowing a boat. In fact, bird flight is much more complicated.

IN THE IMAGE OF A BIRD
Leonardo's notebooks show how intently he studied birds to solve the riddle of flight – and how ingenious he was at devising mechanisms to flap the wings of his machines like a bird's. He thought birds used the tips of their wings to "squeeze" the air and propel them along. So he sketched intricate hinges and pulleys for clenching the wingtips. But he was wrong about wingtips, and never really understood how a bird's wings lift and propel it through the air.

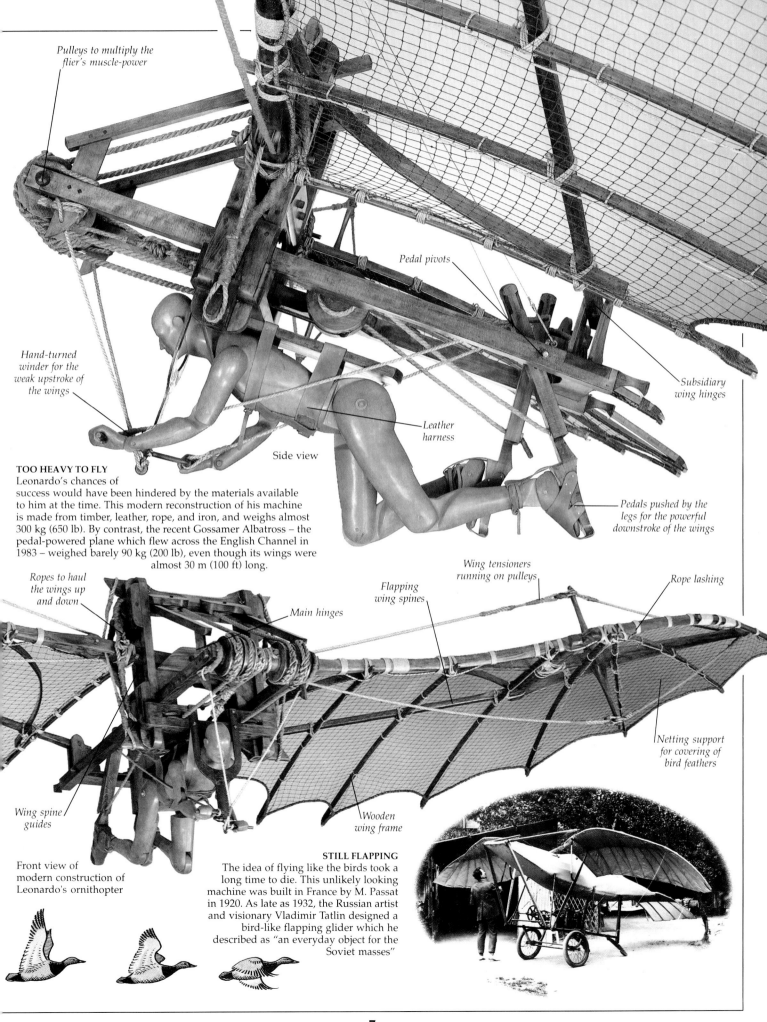

Pulleys to multiply the
flier's muscle-power

Pedal pivots

Hand-turned
winder for the
weak upstroke of
the wings

Subsidiary
wing hinges

Leather
harness

Side view

TOO HEAVY TO FLY
Leonardo's chances of
success would have been hindered by the materials available
to him at the time. This modern reconstruction of his machine
is made from timber, leather, rope, and iron, and weighs almost
300 kg (650 lb). By contrast, the recent Gossamer Albatross – the
pedal-powered plane which flew across the English Channel in
1983 – weighed barely 90 kg (200 lb), even though its wings were
almost 30 m (100 ft) long.

Pedals pushed by the
legs for the powerful
downstroke of the wings

Wing tensioners
running on pulleys

Rope lashing

Ropes to haul
the wings up
and down

Flapping
wing spines

Main hinges

Netting support
for covering of
bird feathers

Wing spine
guides

Wooden
wing frame

Front view of
modern construction of
Leonardo's ornithopter

STILL FLAPPING
The idea of flying like the birds took a
long time to die. This unlikely looking
machine was built in France by M. Passat
in 1920. As late as 1932, the Russian artist
and visionary Vladimir Tatlin designed a
bird-like flapping glider which he
described as "an everyday object for the
Soviet masses"

7

Lighter than air

Hoop or load ring suspended from a net looped over the gas envelope

IT WAS NOT WINGS like a bird's but a bubble of air that carried man aloft for the first time. People had long believed that a balloon filled with a gas that was lighter than air would float in the air like a ship on water. The problem was to find this gas. In fact, the first answer was simply hot air – because hot air is less dense than cool air. In 1783, the French Montgolfier brothers made a huge paper balloon and filled it with hot air. In front of astonished Parisians, it rose majestically into the air, carrying two men. Within a fortnight, a second historic balloon flight was made over Paris, this time by Jacques Charles and M. Robert. Their rubberized silk balloon was filled not with hot air but with hydrogen gas, and this was to prove much more practical.

THE FIRST FLIGHT
On 21 November 1783, Francois de Rozier and the Marquis d'Arlandes became the world's first aeronauts, as the Montgolfier brothers' magnificent blue and gold balloon carried them into the air above Paris.

—Short ropes suspending the basket from the load ring

FANTASTIC!
Over 400,000 people witnessed Charles's and Robert's historic flight, commemorated on this fan.

BALLOON MANIA
Parisian society went "balloon mad" and snapped up mementoes of the new wonder of the age, like this magic-lantern slide. Pulling the inner portion gave the illusion that the balloon was rising.

Strong rail to carry bags of sand ballast which was jettisoned to reduce weight and maintain height

SOCIAL CLIMBING
In the late 19th century, ballooning became a fashionable society sport, and well-to-do gentlemen would compete for distance and height records.

SOFT LANDING
Early balloons often hit the ground with a sickening thud. Some carried wicker cushions strapped below the balloon basket to soften the blow.

GAS BALLOON
Gas ballooning was popular throughout the 19th century because flights could last for hours – unlike hot-air flights, which were over as soon as the air cooled. Gas balloonists had two control lines – one to let out gas through a valve at the top of the balloon, for descending, and another to open the "ripping seam" to deflate the balloon once safely back on the ground.

Airships

The problem with balloons was that they simply floated where the wind took them. So in 1852, Henri Giffard made a cigar-shaped balloon and powered it with a steam engine to make it "dirigible" or steerable. Later, with petrol engines and rigid-framed envelopes, such "airships" were the first large aircraft. By the 1920s, vast airships were carrying people across the Atlantic in ocean-liner-style. But a series of disasters caused by the flammable hydrogen gas spelled the end for airships.

SHIPS IN THE NIGHT
The sight of vast airships looming right over the heart of the city could be awe-inspiring.

ZEPPELIN *below*
The German Zeppelin company led the world in airship-building. But their giant, 245 m (800 ft)-long ship, the *Hindenburg*, was destroyed in a terrible accident in 1937, killing 35 passengers.

The *Hindenburg* and a modern "jumbo jet" to the same scale

RIDING HIGH
Balloon races were immensely popular in the late 1800s. Professional aeronauts would often ride the load ring to make more room in the basket for joy-riding clients.

Pocket barometer c .1909

UP AND DOWN *left*
In order to keep the balloon at a steady altitude, sand ballast had to be jettisoned to make up for the gradual seeping of gas from the envelope. But the balance was delicate. Throwing out too much ballast made the balloon climb, forcing the aeronaut to let out more gas - not only to bring the balloon back down but because the gas expands at higher altitude and has to be vented. Constant venting of gas and jettisoning of ballast cut flights short, so early balloonists always carried sensitive barometric (pressure-controlled) "statoscopes" to tell them whether their balloons were rising or falling.

Statoscope c .1900

STATOSCOPE
J. RICHARD
95.R.MELINGUE
PARIS

Statoscope c .1870

Anchor to tether the balloon during inflation

MAKING GAS
The hydrogen gas to fill balloons was made by dripping sulphuric acid on iron turnings in contraptions like this.

Basket made of wicker for lightness and resilience to landing shocks

GAS DETECTOR
Hydrogen is so flammable that it was vital to know if there were any leaks. This meter detected its presence.

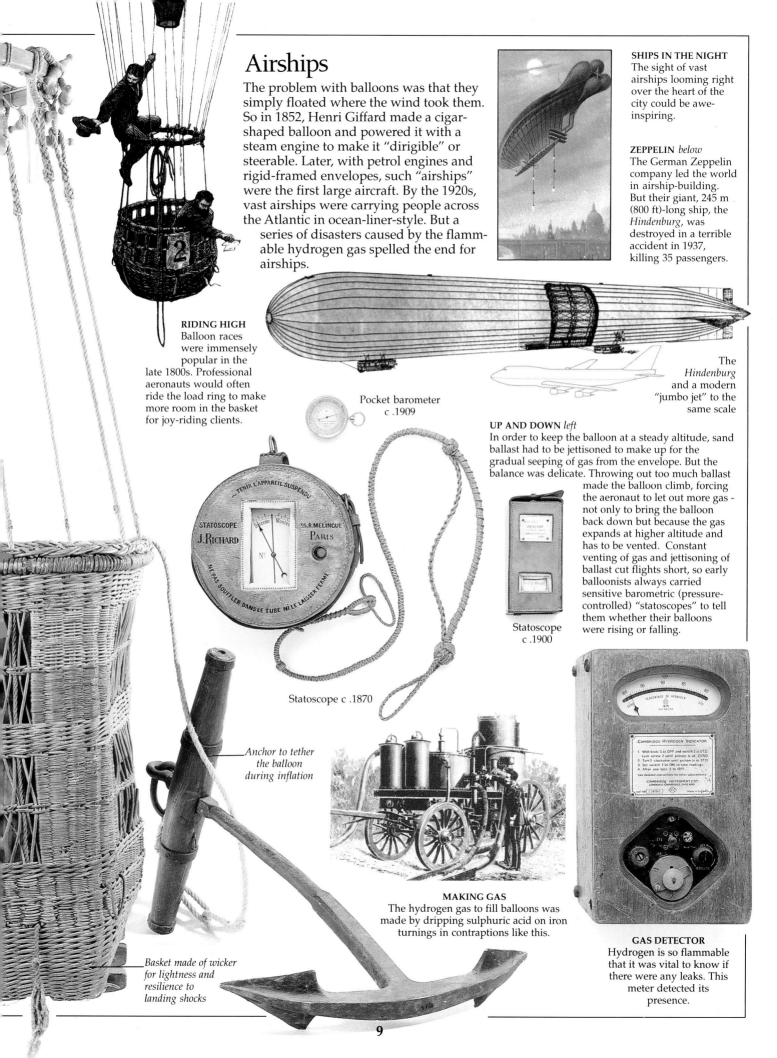

Gliding aloft

FOR A WHILE it seemed the future of flight lay with balloons and lighter-than-air craft. But the British engineer Sir George Cayley, at least, thought otherwise. He was convinced that wings, too, would one day carry people into the air, drawing his inspiration from a familiar plaything, the kite. Ingenious experiments with kites taught Cayley so much about how wings are lifted on the air that he was able to build a man-size version – the world's first real glider. Soon, other would-be aviators were trying their luck with gliders. It was all rather hit-and-miss, though, for no-one had any real idea how to control their craft in the air. Then, in the 1890s, a brave young German called Otto Lilienthal built a series of small, fragile gliders – rather like modern hang-gliders – and succeeded in making regular, controlled flights in them. His example proved crucial, and he has rightly been called the "world's first true aviator".

Tailplane

THE OLDEST AIRCRAFT?
Kites were probably flown in China over 3,000 years ago, and arrived in Europe from there in the 14th century.

HANGING IN THE AIR
Photographs of Lilienthal gliding were published around the world, inspiring many imitators. His approach to flying was very scientific; he studied each problem with an analytical eye and tested each solution critically. Aviators should learn to glide, he insisted, and get "on intimate terms with the air" before taking the risky step of fitting a motor – advice that was crucial to the success of the Wright brothers (p. 12).

Sir George Cayley

Sir George Cayley

The invention of the aeroplane owes a great deal to the pioneering work of the English baronet Sir George Cayley (1773-1857). It was Cayley who first worked out how a wing works, and all modern aircraft are based on the kite-like model glider he built in 1804, with its up-angled front wing and stabilizing tail. In 1853, at the age of 80, he built a full-size glider which is said to have carried his terrified coachman in a flight across a small valley.

PLANE IDEAS *below*
Cayley had ideas for many different flying machines, including an airship and this person-carrying glider, which he called a "governable parachute".

Wing cover of unvarnished cotton

Replica of Lilienthal's No. 11 hang-glider of 1895

Wing moving left to right, with airflow shown in blue and vertical arrow showing lift

HOW A WING WORKS

Wings are lifted by the air flowing above and beneath as they cut through the air. Air pushed over the top speeds up and is stretched out, so that the pressure here drops. But air flowing beneath slows down and pressure rises. So, in effect, the wing is sucked from above and pushed from below. Even a flat board can give some lift, but pioneers like Lilienthal discovered that a curved or "cambered" surface is best. Today, wings are thicker and far more effective than those of the pioneers. Research with computers and wind tunnels ensures the right shape for each type of aircraft.

Wooden spars to keep wing shape

TRAGIC ACCIDENT

Sadly, Lilienthal was killed in 1896 while flying one of his gliders. The accident occurred not in town as suggested by this engraving but in open country near Berlin, when a gust of wind threw the glider out of control.

BRACED PAIR

The Wright brothers (p. 14) adopted the same braced construction as this biplane (double wing) built by French-American Octave Chanute in the mid-1890s.

Willow hoop to act as shock absorber

Lilienthal supported himself on his forearms and controlled the glider by swinging his legs to shift its centre of gravity

BELL'S KITE

Many pioneers believed that huge man-carrying kites had a future. This one was designed by the telephone pioneer Alexander Graham Bell.

Willow ribs

Powered flight

Wᴛʜ ᴀ ɢʟɪᴅᴇʀ, it was at last possible to fly on wings – but not for long. To fly any real distance, an engine was needed. By as early as 1845, two Englishmen, William Henson and John Stringfellow, had built a working model of a plane powered by a specially made lightweight steam engine – the only engine then available. Nobody knows whether their model ever really got off the ground, but it showed that the idea of a powered flying machine was no longer just a dream. Over the next 50 years, many imaginative engineers tried to get steam-powered flying machines air-borne, both models and full-size aeroplanes. But steam engines proved either too weak or too heavy, and it needed the invention of compact, powerful petrol engines for powered flight to become a real possibility.

EAGLE POWER
People had long known that a little more than human power was needed to fly. . .

"All-moving tailplane" or elevator

Silk covered wings with 6 m (20 ft) span

Wing-brace

Rudder

Boiler

Engine pulley

Connecting rod

Steam tube

Cylinder and piston

STEAM POWER
Henson and Stringfellow built a special lightweight steam engine for their model, with a boiler no longer than 25 cm (10 in). Heat for the engine came from a naptha or spirit burner, and steam was raised in the row of conical tubes. (In the full-size version, the boiler would have had 50 of these tubes, but the engine was never built.) Steam from the boiler drove the piston up and down, turning the wooden pulley wheel. This, in turn, spun the two propellers via a twine drive belt.

DID IT FLY?
Stringfellow built another model in 1848. To launch it, he ran it down a sloping wire for 10 m (30 ft) and then released it with the engine running. Some accounts say the model showed true powered flight by climbing a little before it hit a wall.

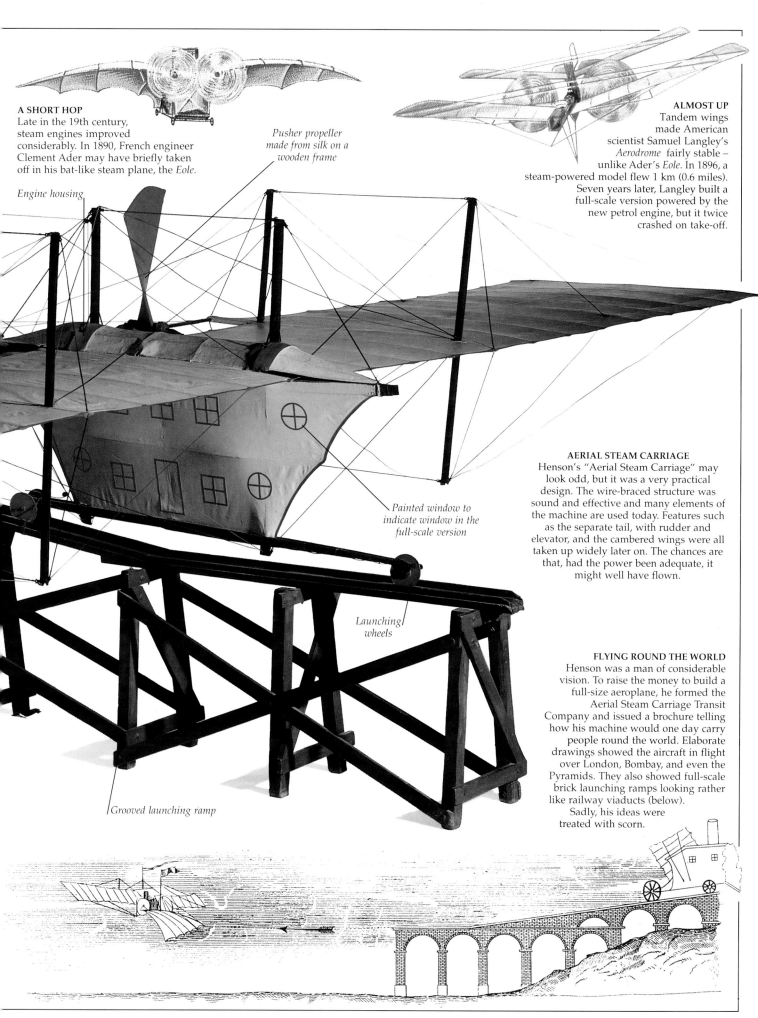

A SHORT HOP
Late in the 19th century, steam engines improved considerably. In 1890, French engineer Clement Ader may have briefly taken off in his bat-like steam plane, the *Eole*.

Engine housing

Pusher propeller made from silk on a wooden frame

ALMOST UP
Tandem wings made American scientist Samuel Langley's *Aerodrome* fairly stable – unlike Ader's *Eole*. In 1896, a steam-powered model flew 1 km (0.6 miles). Seven years later, Langley built a full-scale version powered by the new petrol engine, but it twice crashed on take-off.

Painted window to indicate window in the full-scale version

AERIAL STEAM CARRIAGE
Henson's "Aerial Steam Carriage" may look odd, but it was a very practical design. The wire-braced structure was sound and effective and many elements of the machine are used today. Features such as the separate tail, with rudder and elevator, and the cambered wings were all taken up widely later on. The chances are that, had the power been adequate, it might well have flown.

Launching wheels

FLYING ROUND THE WORLD
Henson was a man of considerable vision. To raise the money to build a full-size aeroplane, he formed the Aerial Steam Carriage Transit Company and issued a brochure telling how his machine would one day carry people round the world. Elaborate drawings showed the aircraft in flight over London, Bombay, and even the Pyramids. They also showed full-scale brick launching ramps looking rather like railway viaducts (below).
Sadly, his ideas were treated with scorn.

Grooved launching ramp

13

The first aeroplanes

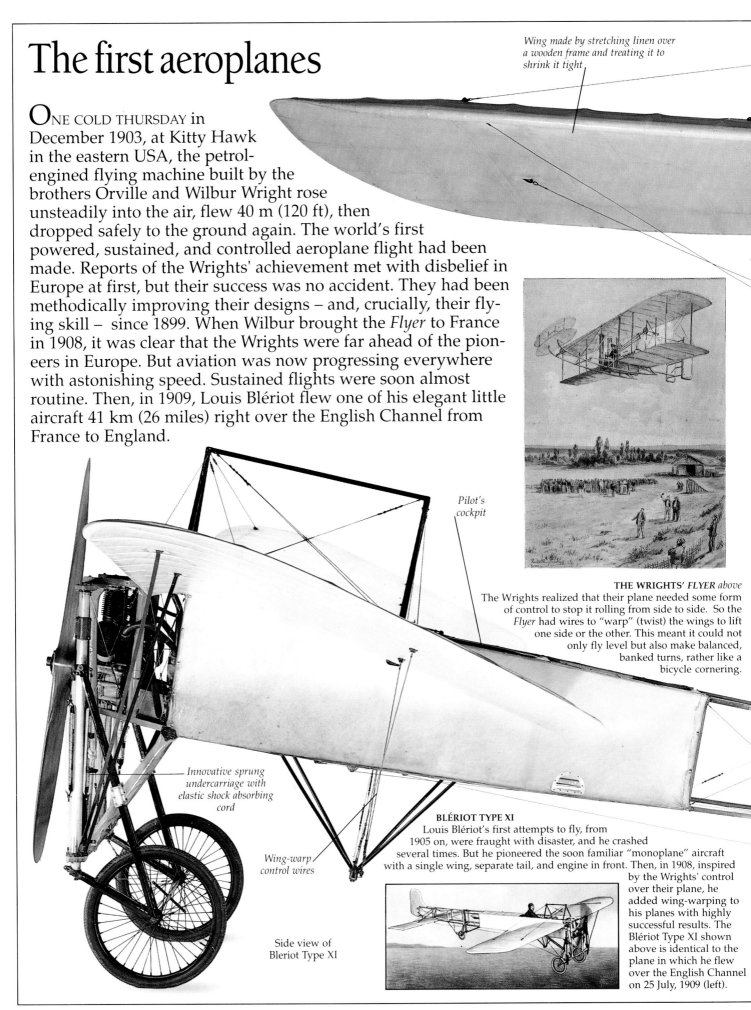

Wing made by stretching linen over a wooden frame and treating it to shrink it tight

ONE COLD THURSDAY in December 1903, at Kitty Hawk in the eastern USA, the petrol-engined flying machine built by the brothers Orville and Wilbur Wright rose unsteadily into the air, flew 40 m (120 ft), then dropped safely to the ground again. The world's first powered, sustained, and controlled aeroplane flight had been made. Reports of the Wrights' achievement met with disbelief in Europe at first, but their success was no accident. They had been methodically improving their designs – and, crucially, their flying skill – since 1899. When Wilbur brought the *Flyer* to France in 1908, it was clear that the Wrights were far ahead of the pioneers in Europe. But aviation was now progressing everywhere with astonishing speed. Sustained flights were soon almost routine. Then, in 1909, Louis Blériot flew one of his elegant little aircraft 41 km (26 miles) right over the English Channel from France to England.

Pilot's cockpit

THE WRIGHTS' *FLYER* *above*
The Wrights realized that their plane needed some form of control to stop it rolling from side to side. So the *Flyer* had wires to "warp" (twist) the wings to lift one side or the other. This meant it could not only fly level but also make balanced, banked turns, rather like a bicycle cornering.

Innovative sprung undercarriage with elastic shock absorbing cord

Wing-warp control wires

BLÉRIOT TYPE XI
Louis Blériot's first attempts to fly, from 1905 on, were fraught with disaster, and he crashed several times. But he pioneered the soon familiar "monoplane" aircraft with a single wing, separate tail, and engine in front. Then, in 1908, inspired by the Wrights' control over their plane, he added wing-warping to his planes with highly successful results. The Blériot Type XI shown above is identical to the plane in which he flew over the English Channel on 25 July, 1909 (left).

Side view of Bleriot Type XI

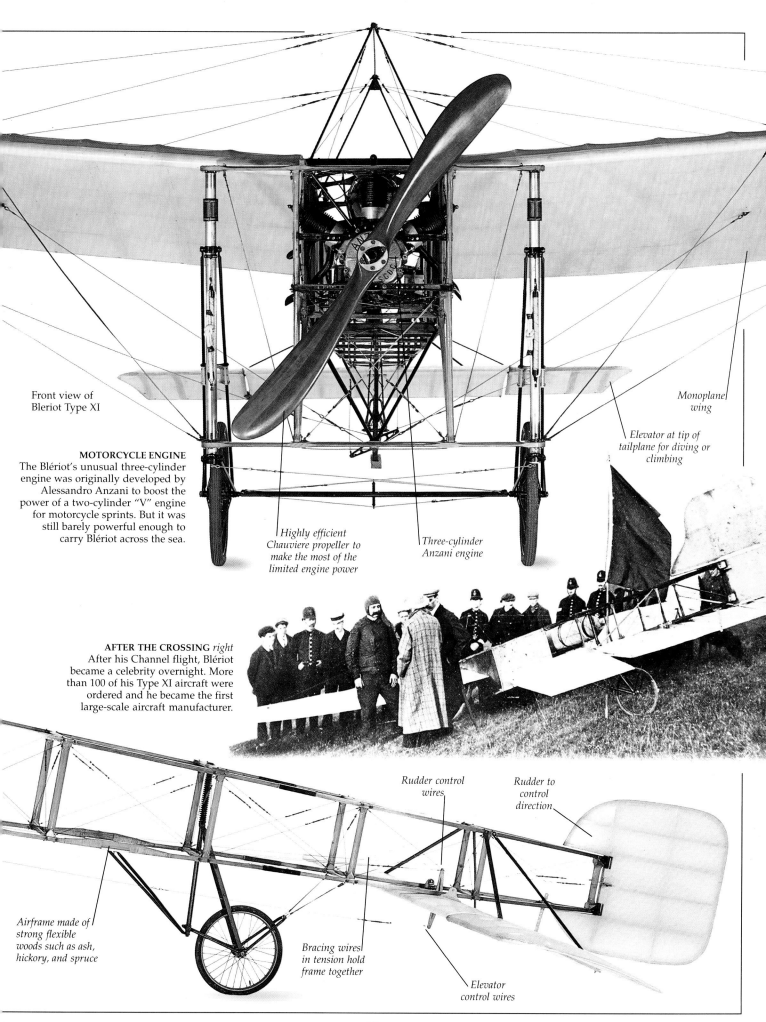

Front view of
Bleriot Type XI

MOTORCYCLE ENGINE
The Blériot's unusual three-cylinder
engine was originally developed by
Alessandro Anzani to boost the
power of a two-cylinder "V" engine
for motorcycle sprints. But it was
still barely powerful enough to
carry Blériot across the sea.

*Highly efficient
Chauviere propeller to
make the most of the
limited engine power*

*Three-cylinder
Anzani engine*

*Monoplane
wing*

*Elevator at tip of
tailplane for diving or
climbing*

AFTER THE CROSSING *right*
After his Channel flight, Blériot
became a celebrity overnight. More
than 100 of his Type XI aircraft were
ordered and he became the first
large-scale aircraft manufacturer.

*Rudder control
wires*

*Rudder to
control
direction*

*Airframe made of
strong flexible
woods such as ash,
hickory, and spruce*

*Bracing wires
in tension hold
frame together*

*Elevator
control wires*

Those magnificent men

THE FEATS OF THE WRIGHTS, Blériot, and various other brave and inventive pioneers created tremendous excitement, and aviation emerged as the sensation of the age. The daring young men who demonstrated their flying skill at air displays quickly became superstars. When a Parisian theatre audience found in its midst Adolphe Pégoud – one of the first pilots to display aerobatics and loops – they stopped the show until he gave them a talk on aviation! Another pioneer pilot, Louis Paulhan, was said to have earned over one million francs from his flying exploits. The early fliers certainly earned their fame, for their planes were difficult and dangerous to fly and accidents were frequent. Sitting on an exposed seat was also uncomfortable and very, very cold. Warm clothing was absolutely vital. When Blériot crossed the Channel, he wore a boiler suit, but special flying gear was soon developed.

Soft "chrome" leather

FINDING THE WAY
In the early days, pilots navigated by flying straight towards landmarks. A good set of maps was invaluable.

Warm wool lining

HOT FOOT
Warm boots were essential. These are soft sheepskin-lined "fug" boots, originally thigh-length but cut down by the owner for convenience.

Thick rubber sole gave good grip when climbing aboard the aircraft

"WINDPROOF AIRMAN KIT"
This suit from around 1911 could be lined with either fleece or quilt.

Flying gear c. 1916

World War I spurred the rapid development of flying gear. This selection was issued to pilots of the British Royal Flying Corps. Leather was thought the best material at the time, but was soon replaced by one-piece "Sidcot" suits of waxed cotton lined with silk and fur.

Fold-up collar to keep neck warm

Goggle-holders

HEAD IN THE CLOUDS
Cowl-type helmets with face masks like this were sometimes used for high-altitude flying. But some "aces" felt more alert flying without either helmet or goggles.

GOGGLE-EYED
For most pilots, goggles gave vital eye protection against the wind. This pair is tinted to reduce glare and made with anti-splinter glass.

Leather gloves lined with sheepskin mitten

HANDS IN THE AIR
Stuck out in the airstream on the controls, hands could quickly suffer frostbite if not protected by warm gloves.

Button-up cuffs to keep out wind

WINDPROOF
Higher speeds and longer flights in World War I meant suits had to be more windproof, particularly at the neck, wrists, and ankles.

Double wings

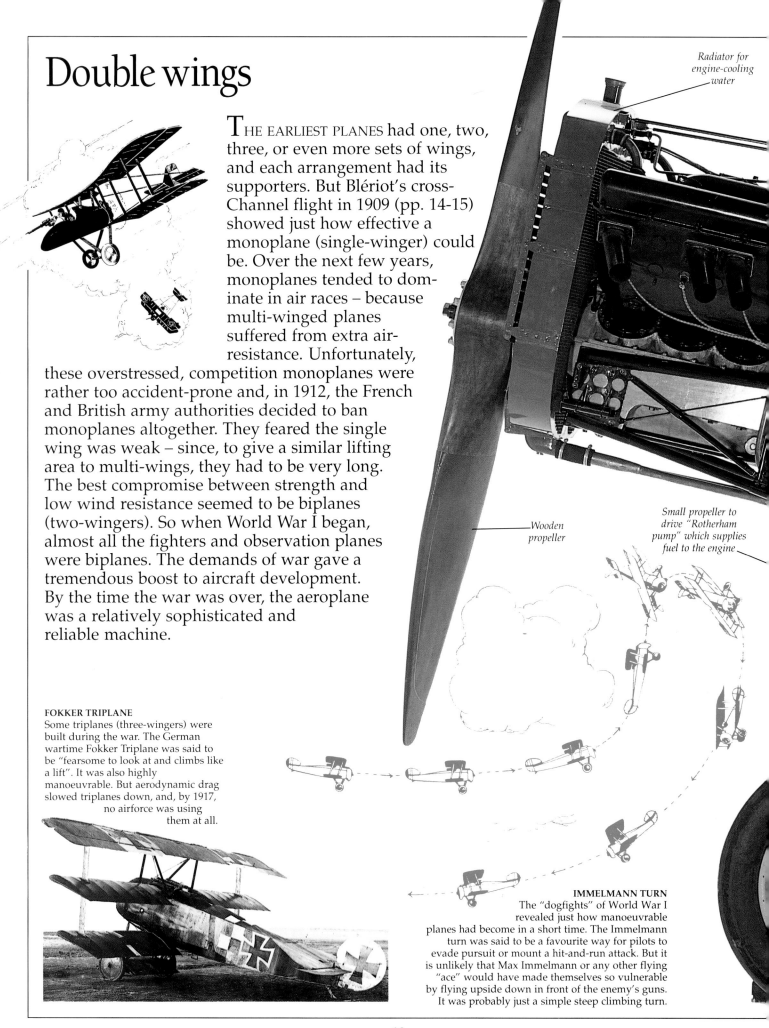

THE EARLIEST PLANES had one, two, three, or even more sets of wings, and each arrangement had its supporters. But Blériot's cross-Channel flight in 1909 (pp. 14-15) showed just how effective a monoplane (single-winger) could be. Over the next few years, monoplanes tended to dominate in air races – because multi-winged planes suffered from extra air-resistance. Unfortunately, these overstressed, competition monoplanes were rather too accident-prone and, in 1912, the French and British army authorities decided to ban monoplanes altogether. They feared the single wing was weak – since, to give a similar lifting area to multi-wings, they had to be very long. The best compromise between strength and low wind resistance seemed to be biplanes (two-wingers). So when World War I began, almost all the fighters and observation planes were biplanes. The demands of war gave a tremendous boost to aircraft development. By the time the war was over, the aeroplane was a relatively sophisticated and reliable machine.

Radiator for engine-cooling water

Wooden propeller

Small propeller to drive "Rotherham pump" which supplies fuel to the engine

FOKKER TRIPLANE
Some triplanes (three-wingers) were built during the war. The German wartime Fokker Triplane was said to be "fearsome to look at and climbs like a lift". It was also highly manoeuvrable. But aerodynamic drag slowed triplanes down, and, by 1917, no airforce was using them at all.

IMMELMANN TURN
The "dogfights" of World War I revealed just how manoeuvrable planes had become in a short time. The Immelmann turn was said to be a favourite way for pilots to evade pursuit or mount a hit-and-run attack. But it is unlikely that Max Immelmann or any other flying "ace" would have made themselves so vulnerable by flying upside down in front of the enemy's guns. It was probably just a simple steep climbing turn.

8-cylinder 300 hp
Hispano-Suiza "V"
engine

Vickers forward-firing
machine gun aimed through
a hole in the radiator

Timing device to
ensure gun fires
through the propeller
only when the blades
are horizontal

Control stick for
climbing, diving,
and banking

FIGHTING LIKE DOGS
"Dogfights" were fought
between single-seat Scout
planes with forward-firing
machine guns. Since the pilot
had to aim the whole aircraft
at the enemy to shoot, flying
skill was vital.

Pilot's seat

Rudder
control
wires

Rudder bar

Fuel tank

Ash
frame

Bracing struts

Light wire
landing wheels

Wing stubs

Bristol Fighter
c. 1917

In the early years of the war, the
dangerous work of artillery
spotting and observation
was performed by
slow two-seaters,
often protected
by faster single-
seaters. When
the British Bristol
Fighter came on
the scene in 1917,
however, its powerful
engine made it fast enough
to act as both spotter and fighter.

Continued on next page

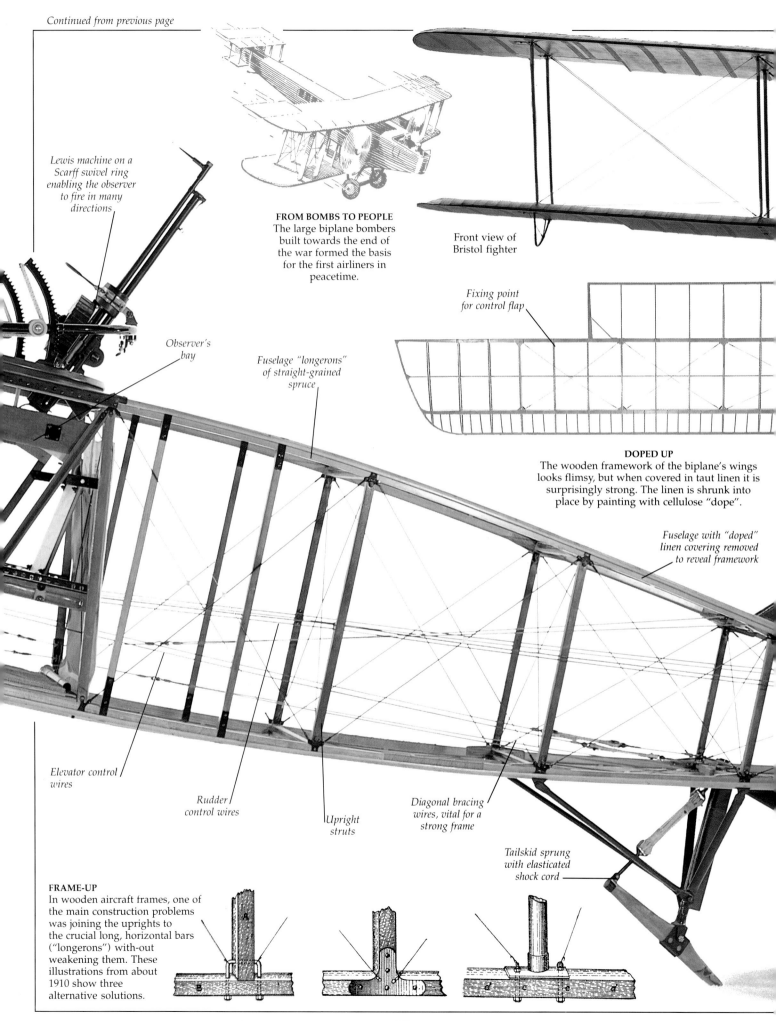

Lewis machine on a Scarff swivel ring enabling the observer to fire in many directions

FROM BOMBS TO PEOPLE
The large biplane bombers built towards the end of the war formed the basis for the first airliners in peacetime.

Front view of Bristol fighter

Fixing point for control flap

DOPED UP
The wooden framework of the biplane's wings looks flimsy, but when covered in taut linen it is surprisingly strong. The linen is shrunk into place by painting with cellulose "dope".

Fuselage with "doped" linen covering removed to reveal framework

Observer's bay

Fuselage "longerons" of straight-grained spruce

Elevator control wires

Rudder control wires

Upright struts

Diagonal bracing wires, vital for a strong frame

Tailskid sprung with elasticated shock cord

FRAME-UP
In wooden aircraft frames, one of the main construction problems was joining the uprights to the crucial long, horizontal bars ("longerons") with-out weakening them. These illustrations from about 1910 show three alternative solutions.

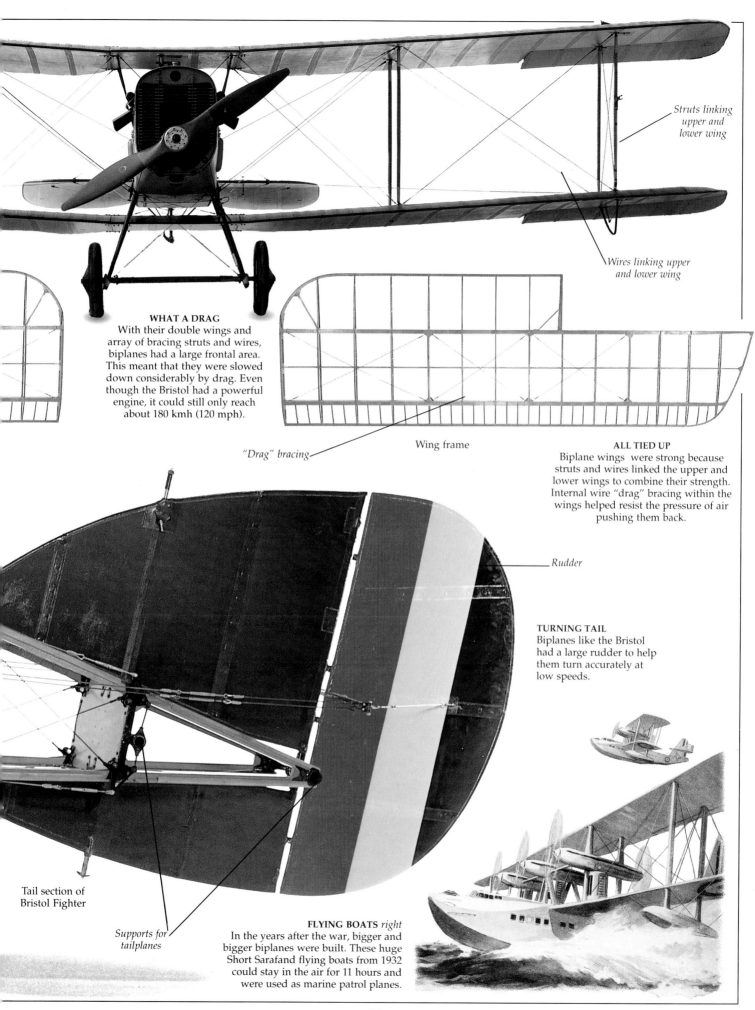

Struts linking upper and lower wing

Wires linking upper and lower wing

WHAT A DRAG
With their double wings and array of bracing struts and wires, biplanes had a large frontal area. This meant that they were slowed down considerably by drag. Even though the Bristol had a powerful engine, it could still only reach about 180 kmh (120 mph).

"Drag" bracing

Wing frame

ALL TIED UP
Biplane wings were strong because struts and wires linked the upper and lower wings to combine their strength. Internal wire "drag" bracing within the wings helped resist the pressure of air pushing them back.

Rudder

TURNING TAIL
Biplanes like the Bristol had a large rudder to help them turn accurately at low speeds.

Tail section of Bristol Fighter

Supports for tailplanes

FLYING BOATS *right*
In the years after the war, bigger and bigger biplanes were built. These huge Short Sarafand flying boats from 1932 could stay in the air for 11 hours and were used as marine patrol planes.

The evolving plane

IN THE 20 YEARS after the first international airshow was held at Reims in France in August 1909, aviation progressed at an astonishing rate. The aeroplanes of 1909 were mostly frail, slow machines with flimsy, open, wood frames, low-powered engines and rudimentary controls. No plane at the airshow flew faster than 75 kmh (47 mph) nor climbed higher than 150 m (500 ft) or so above the ground. Yet, within four years, aircraft were flying over 200 kmh (120 mph), climbing to 6000 m (20,000 ft) and performing aerobatic feats such as loops and rolls (p. 41). By 1929, ungainly wooden planes were almost a thing of the past, and new all-metal planes with streamlined fuselages and wings were tearing across the sky at previously undreamed of speeds.

DEPERDUSSIN 1909
Deperdussin were among the most advanced aircraft manufacturers in the years before World War I, and their sleek monoplanes took many speed records. Nevertheless, this example shows many features typical of the pioneering planes, with lateral control by wing-warping, (p. 14), a low-powered engine, and extensive wire bracing.

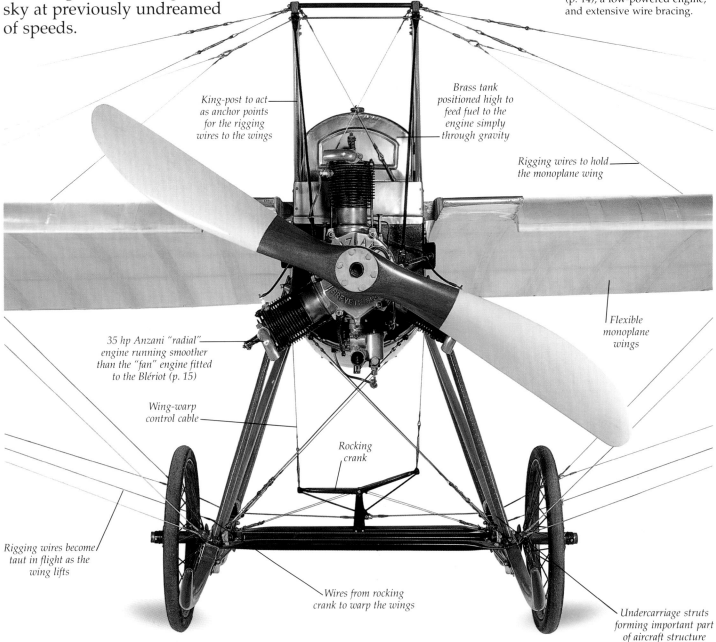

King-post to act as anchor points for the rigging wires to the wings

Brass tank positioned high to feed fuel to the engine simply through gravity

Rigging wires to hold the monoplane wing

35 hp Anzani "radial" engine running smoother than the "fan" engine fitted to the Blériot (p. 15)

Flexible monoplane wings

Wing-warp control cable

Rocking crank

Rigging wires become taut in flight as the wing lifts

Wires from rocking crank to warp the wings

Undercarriage struts forming important part of aircraft structure

SOPWITH PUP 1917

Aircraft improved immeasurably in the years before World War I, and wartime biplane fighters were faster and much more manoeuvrable than the flying machines of the pioneers. Lightweight rotary engines (pp. 28-29) propelled fighters like this Sopwith Pup along at speeds of 185 kmh (115 mph) or more, and improved control allowed them to engage in dramatic aerial dogfights. To bank the plane, the pilot no longer warped the wings but raised or lowered hinged flaps called "ailerons" on the tips of strong, rigid wings (pp. 40-41). Fuselages, by now, were always enclosed and, towards the end of the war, a few aircraft manufacturers began to experiment with "monocoques" in which all the strength came from a single shell rather than internal struts and bracing.

Ailerons

BABY CAMEL
Sopwith were famous for their fighter scout planes in World War I, and the Sopwith Pup (above) was the forerunner of the agile Camel, the most formidable fighter of the war.

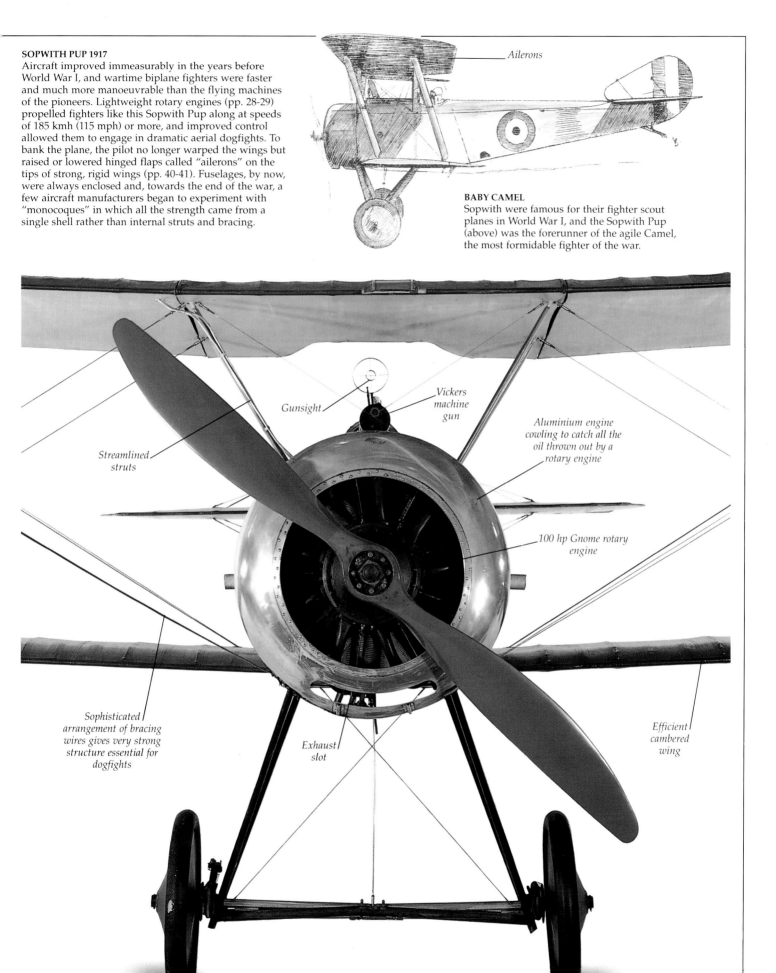

Gunsight

Vickers machine gun

Aluminium engine cowling to catch all the oil thrown out by a rotary engine

Streamlined struts

100 hp Gnome rotary engine

Sophisticated arrangement of bracing wires gives very strong structure essential for dogfights

Exhaust slot

Efficient cambered wing

Continued on next page

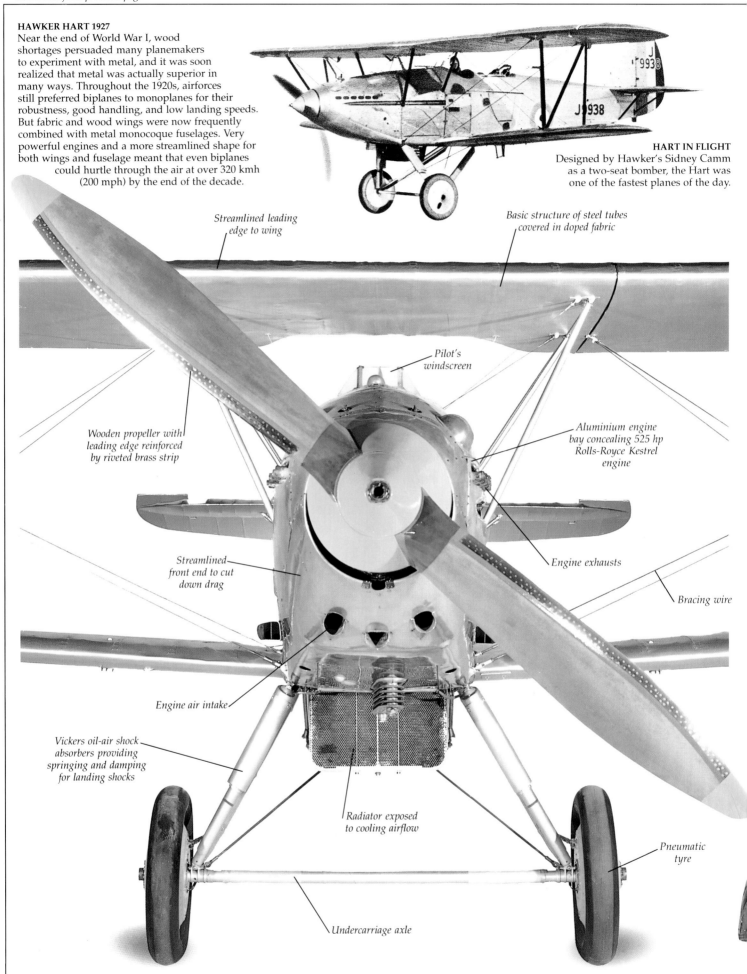

HAWKER HART 1927
Near the end of World War I, wood
shortages persuaded many planemakers
to experiment with metal, and it was soon
realized that metal was actually superior in
many ways. Throughout the 1920s, airforces
still preferred biplanes to monoplanes for their
robustness, good handling, and low landing speeds.
But fabric and wood wings were now frequently
combined with metal monocoque fuselages. Very
powerful engines and a more streamlined shape for
both wings and fuselage meant that even biplanes
could hurtle through the air at over 320 kmh
(200 mph) by the end of the decade.

HART IN FLIGHT
Designed by Hawker's Sidney Camm
as a two-seat bomber, the Hart was
one of the fastest planes of the day.

*Streamlined leading
edge to wing*

*Basic structure of steel tubes
covered in doped fabric*

*Pilot's
windscreen*

*Aluminium engine
bay concealing 525 hp
Rolls-Royce Kestrel
engine*

*Wooden propeller with
leading edge reinforced
by riveted brass strip*

Engine exhausts

*Streamlined
front end to cut
down drag*

Bracing wire

Engine air intake

*Vickers oil-air shock
absorbers providing
springing and damping
for landing shocks*

*Radiator exposed
to cooling airflow*

*Pneumatic
tyre*

Undercarriage axle

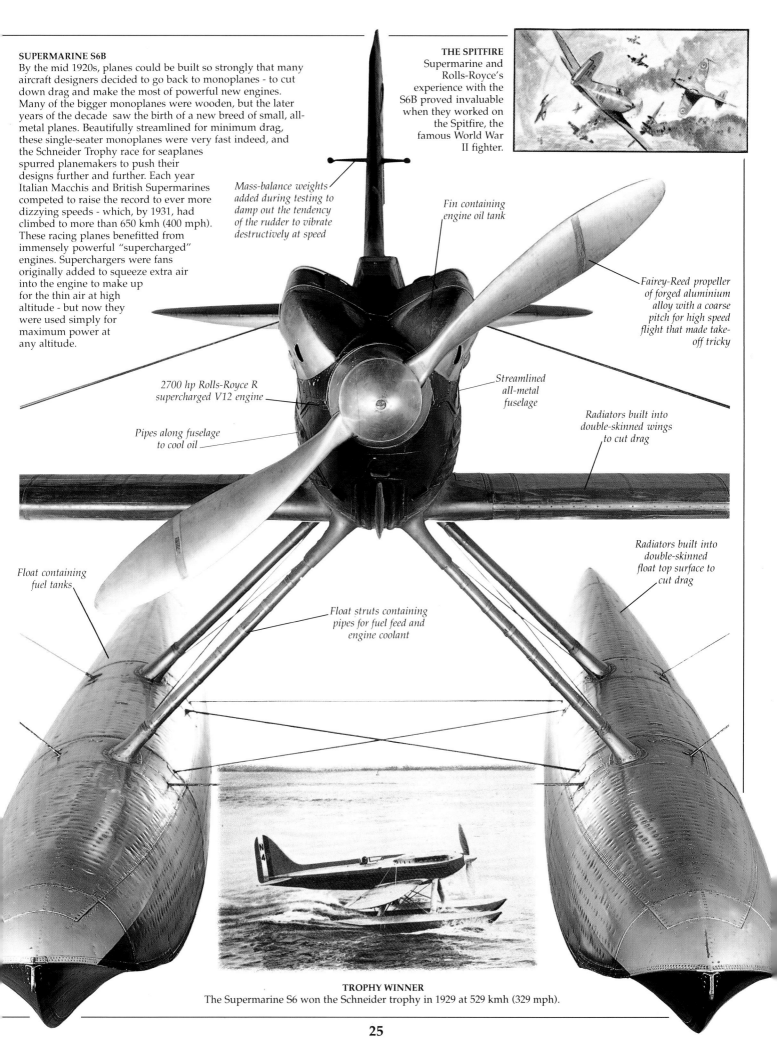

SUPERMARINE S6B

By the mid 1920s, planes could be built so strongly that many aircraft designers decided to go back to monoplanes - to cut down drag and make the most of powerful new engines. Many of the bigger monoplanes were wooden, but the later years of the decade saw the birth of a new breed of small, all-metal planes. Beautifully streamlined for minimum drag, these single-seater monoplanes were very fast indeed, and the Schneider Trophy race for seaplanes spurred planemakers to push their designs further and further. Each year Italian Macchis and British Supermarines competed to raise the record to ever more dizzying speeds - which, by 1931, had climbed to more than 650 kmh (400 mph). These racing planes benefitted from immensely powerful "supercharged" engines. Superchargers were fans originally added to squeeze extra air into the engine to make up for the thin air at high altitude - but now they were used simply for maximum power at any altitude.

THE SPITFIRE
Supermarine and Rolls-Royce's experience with the S6B proved invaluable when they worked on the Spitfire, the famous World War II fighter.

Mass-balance weights added during testing to damp out the tendency of the rudder to vibrate destructively at speed

Fin containing engine oil tank

Fairey-Reed propeller of forged aluminium alloy with a coarse pitch for high speed flight that made take-off tricky

2700 hp Rolls-Royce R supercharged V12 engine

Streamlined all-metal fuselage

Radiators built into double-skinned wings to cut drag

Pipes along fuselage to cool oil

Radiators built into double-skinned float top surface to cut drag

Float containing fuel tanks

Float struts containing pipes for fuel feed and engine coolant

TROPHY WINNER
The Supermarine S6 won the Schneider trophy in 1929 at 529 kmh (329 mph).

Light aircraft

SINGLE-ENGINED LIGHT PLANES are today flown all over the world for training pilots, for basic transport in remote places and for the sheer pleasure of flying. They are very simple aircraft with, typically, a fixed undercarriage, a monoplane wing above the cabin, simple fuselage and tail, and a small petrol engine to turn the propeller at the front. Usually very conventional in design, they work in much the same way as the planes of the pioneers. Only the materials are genuinely new, with aluminium alloys and plastics replacing the traditional wood and linen.

EPIC FLIGHT
The most famous light plane was the *Spirit of St Louis* in which Charles Lindbergh flew solo across the Atlantic in 1927.

Fuel tank holding enough fuel for 2.5 hours or 190 km (120 miles) flying

Tiny, two-cylinder, Rotax engine

SNOWBIRD
The basic shape of light planes has changed little since World War II, and the main elements of planes like the Snowbird have long been familiar to pilots. However, the Snowbird makes the most of modern developments in "microlights" (pp. 62-63). The result is a plane that is not only very light but costs little more than a family car.

PETROL POWER
While bigger, faster planes now usually have jet engines, petrol engines are quite adequate for light planes.

Cabin superstructure of light aluminium, with roof forming wing mounts

Fixed undercarriage

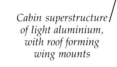

ON THE PANEL
On the Snowbird's instrument panel, digital electronic displays replace the clocks and cables traditionally used on light planes.

Wingfront of alloy sheet in "D box" shape to resist twisting

WEIGHTLIFTER
Wings are specially designed for each plane to give just the right amount of lift; the length of the wing (its "span") and its cross-section ("camber") are critical. Wings must also be light and very strong too. The stresses placed on the wings of even the lightest, slowest plane, as it flies through the air, are considerable. The Snowbird's wing of fabric stretched over an aluminium frame is unusually simple. But the cross-struts and bracing pieces had to be very carefully designed.

Absence of ailerons makes wing frame very simple

AIR SCREW
Most light planes have a traditional twin-bladed propeller of laminated wood, mounted at the front to pull the plane forwards.

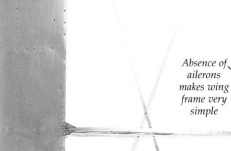

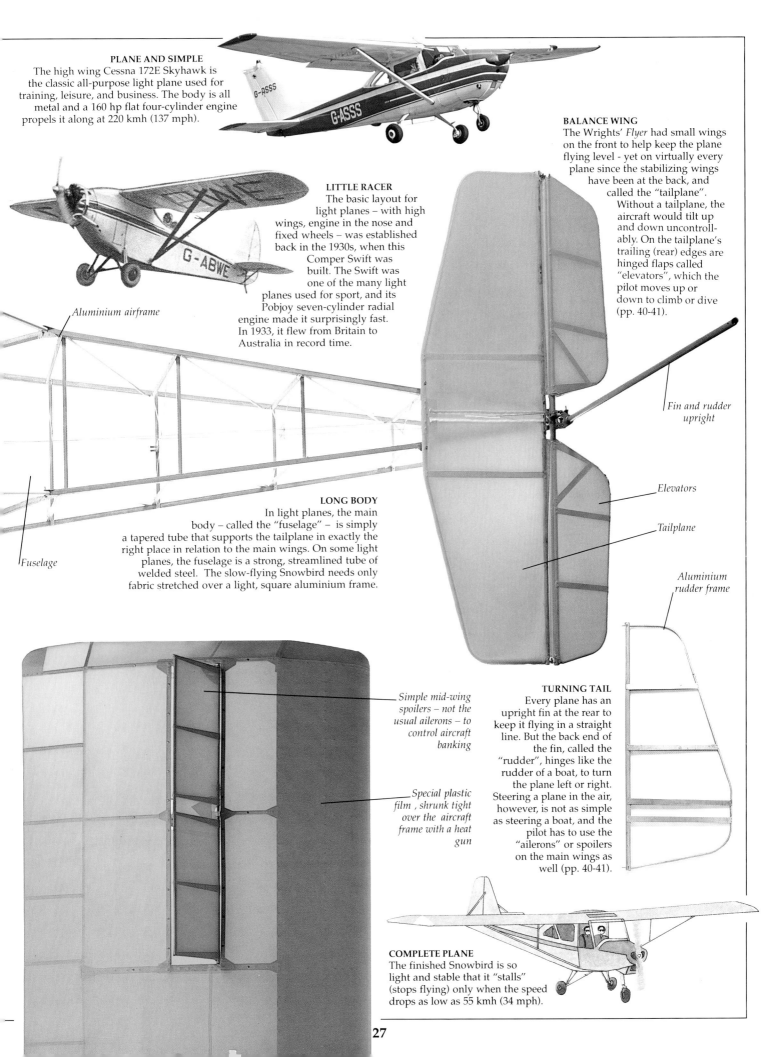

PLANE AND SIMPLE
The high wing Cessna 172E Skyhawk is the classic all-purpose light plane used for training, leisure, and business. The body is all metal and a 160 hp flat four-cylinder engine propels it along at 220 kmh (137 mph).

BALANCE WING
The Wrights' *Flyer* had small wings on the front to help keep the plane flying level - yet on virtually every plane since the stabilizing wings have been at the back, and called the "tailplane". Without a tailplane, the aircraft would tilt up and down uncontrollably. On the tailplane's trailing (rear) edges are hinged flaps called "elevators", which the pilot moves up or down to climb or dive (pp. 40-41).

LITTLE RACER
The basic layout for light planes – with high wings, engine in the nose and fixed wheels – was established back in the 1930s, when this Comper Swift was built. The Swift was one of the many light planes used for sport, and its Pobjoy seven-cylinder radial engine made it surprisingly fast. In 1933, it flew from Britain to Australia in record time.

Aluminium airframe

Fin and rudder upright

Elevators

Tailplane

LONG BODY
In light planes, the main body – called the "fuselage" – is simply a tapered tube that supports the tailplane in exactly the right place in relation to the main wings. On some light planes, the fuselage is a strong, streamlined tube of welded steel. The slow-flying Snowbird needs only fabric stretched over a light, square aluminium frame.

Fuselage

Aluminium rudder frame

Simple mid-wing spoilers – not the usual ailerons – to control aircraft banking

Special plastic film , shrunk tight over the aircraft frame with a heat gun

TURNING TAIL
Every plane has an upright fin at the rear to keep it flying in a straight line. But the back end of the fin, called the "rudder", hinges like the rudder of a boat, to turn the plane left or right. Steering a plane in the air, however, is not as simple as steering a boat, and the pilot has to use the "ailerons" or spoilers on the main wings as well (pp. 40-41).

COMPLETE PLANE
The finished Snowbird is so light and stable that it "stalls" (stops flying) only when the speed drops as low as 55 kmh (34 mph).

Aero-engines

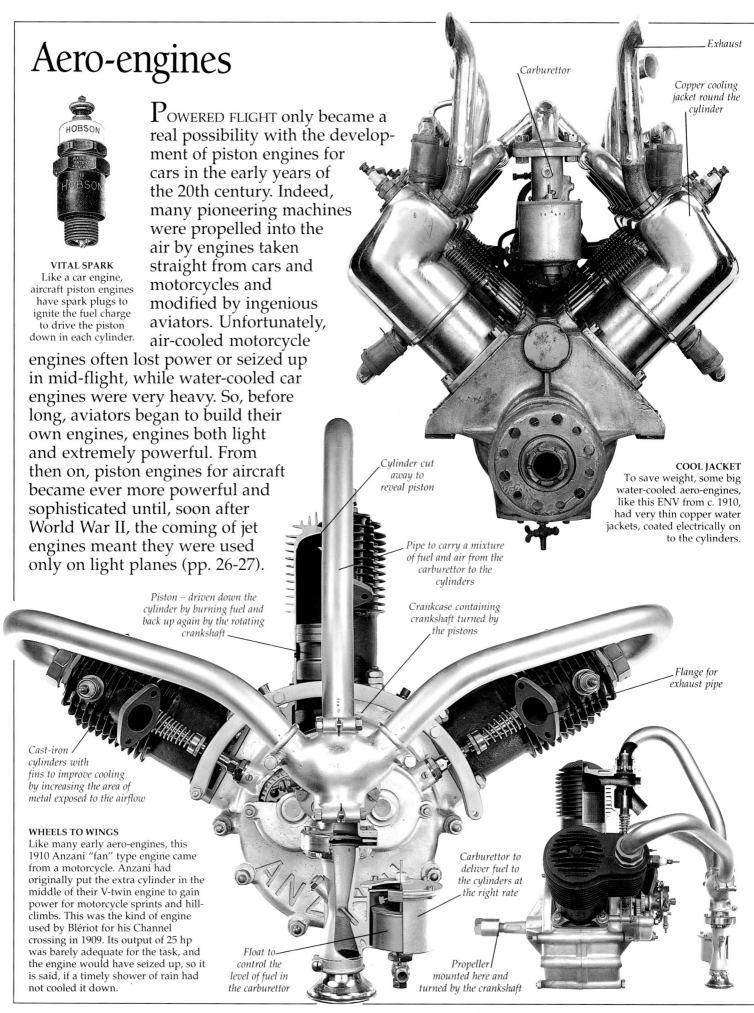

POWERED FLIGHT only became a real possibility with the development of piston engines for cars in the early years of the 20th century. Indeed, many pioneering machines were propelled into the air by engines taken straight from cars and motorcycles and modified by ingenious aviators. Unfortunately, air-cooled motorcycle engines often lost power or seized up in mid-flight, while water-cooled car engines were very heavy. So, before long, aviators began to build their own engines, engines both light and extremely powerful. From then on, piston engines for aircraft became ever more powerful and sophisticated until, soon after World War II, the coming of jet engines meant they were used only on light planes (pp. 26-27).

Carburettor

Exhaust

Copper cooling jacket round the cylinder

COOL JACKET
To save weight, some big water-cooled aero-engines, like this ENV from c. 1910, had very thin copper water jackets, coated electrically on to the cylinders.

Cylinder cut away to reveal piston

Pipe to carry a mixture of fuel and air from the carburettor to the cylinders

Crankcase containing crankshaft turned by the pistons

Piston – driven down the cylinder by burning fuel and back up again by the rotating crankshaft

Flange for exhaust pipe

Cast-iron cylinders with fins to improve cooling by increasing the area of metal exposed to the airflow

WHEELS TO WINGS
Like many early aero-engines, this 1910 Anzani "fan" type engine came from a motorcycle. Anzani had originally put the extra cylinder in the middle of their V-twin engine to gain power for motorcycle sprints and hill-climbs. This was the kind of engine used by Blériot for his Channel crossing in 1909. Its output of 25 hp was barely adequate for the task, and the engine would have seized up, so it is said, if a timely shower of rain had not cooled it down.

Carburettor to deliver fuel to the cylinders at the right rate

Float to control the level of fuel in the carburettor

Propeller mounted here and turned by the crankshaft

ROTARY ENGINE
The earliest aero-engines had cylinders either in-line and needed heavy water-cooling systems, or in a circle (radially) and did not cool well at all. So in 1909, the French Seguin brothers brought in the "rotary" engine. Like the radial engine, it had the cylinders in a ring. But, unlike the radial, the cylinders all went round with the propeller while the central crank stayed still.

Crankshaft, which alone stays still while the cylinders rotate around it

Inlet pipes channelling the fuel and air mixture from the crankcase to the cylinders

Valves to let fuel in and burned gases (exhaust) out

Cylinders kept especially cool by the flow of air around them as they rotate

Crank case rotates with the cylinders

Finely machined cylinders with light, thin walls only 1 mm thick

AERO-GIANT
Not all propeller planes were powered by piston engines. The huge Saunders Roe Princess flying-boat had six big "turboprop" jet engines (p. 36) to turn twelve propellers.

Connecting rods to pistons all joined to a single bearing around the crankshaft

LIGHT POWER
Piston engines for light planes are now very light and compact. This Weslake weighs only 8.4 kg (18 lb) – yet pushes out as much power as Blériot's 1908 Anzani which weighed over 70 kg (150 lb).

Carburettor

Propeller shaft

Cylinder

The propeller

PROPELLERS seem to have changed little since the pioneering days. Yet, as the Wright brothers were quick to appreciate, they are not simply oars for the air; they are like spinning wings that thrust the plane forwards in much the same way as wings lift it upwards. So the shape of a propeller is as crucial to performance as the shape of a wing, and the subtle evolution of propeller design over the years has improved efficiency dramatically. They have gained in strength, too, as construction has changed from "laminations" (layers) of wood to forged aluminium, to cope with steadily increasing engine power.

WRIGHT 1909
The Wright brothers built their own wind tunnel for testing wings and propellers. This design shows they knew that the blade had to be twisted to give it a shallower angle at the tip.

PHILLIPS 1893
This early propeller, designed by "aerofoil" (wing shape) expert Horatio Phillips, looks rather like a ship's screw. Yet it worked well, once lifting a tethered experimental aircraft weighing 180 kg (400 lb).

Propeller blade made up from strips of wood

Blade angle (pitch) steeper closer to the hub

Tip travels farther and faster than hub

Propeller rotates this way

Hub

Leading edge

Trailing edge

PARAGON 1909
The profile of this experimental blade is good but there was no need for such a sweeping shape at the slow spinning speeds of the time.

PITCH AND TWIST
The thrust developed by a propeller varies with its speed and the angle at which its blades carve through the air – its pitch. Because the propeller tip spins faster than the hub, the blade is twisted to make the pitch steep near the hub but shallower towards the tip. This keeps thrust even all the way along the blade.

Brass cover to protect the blade from sea spray

LANG 1917
Long and robust, this laminated propeller was made to cope with the power of a 225 hp Sunbeam engine on a Short 184 seaplane. The brass-clad tips protect it from erosion by sea spray.

WOTAN 1917
The laminated construction is clearly visible in this elegant German propeller. The propeller was made by glueing roughly shaped laminations together and then carving them to form a smoothly tapered aerofoil.

EXTRA BLADES
As engine power increased, propellers were made with three or four blades to cope with the extra load.

Rivets to hold the brass armour to the blade

Laminations of spruce and ash

Swivel to vary the pitch of the blades

HELE-SHAW-BEACHAM 1928
Ideally, an aircraft needs coarse (steeply) pitched propellers for cruising at speed and fine (shallow) pitch for good thrust at take-off. So in the late 1920s, many aircraft began using propellers on which the angle of the blades could be changed to suit the conditions. This particular "variable pitch" propeller was operated by engine oil pressure.

FAIREY-REED 1922
As aircraft designers tried to get planes to go faster and faster in the years after World War I, so they demanded thinner blades to slice easily through the air. But thin wooden blades were too weak to take the strain. In 1920, S.A. Reed developed a way of making strong forged aluminium propellers. Over the years, these gradually displaced laminated wooden propellers.

INTEGRALE 1919
The brass sheath covering this wooden-bladed propeller was designed to protect it from enemy attack. Before interruptor gear was invented (pp. 18-19), propellers on some French fighter planes had even heavier armour-plating to stop them being destroyed by their own forward-firing machine-gun.

Swivelling blade to give the right pitch for both landing and high-speed cruising

UNDUCTED FAN 1986
To save fuel, jet engine manufacturers have recently adopted propellers once again – only now they are called "unducted fans" and spin on the rear of jet engines.

Flying the world

THE TIME BETWEEN THE TWO WORLD WARS was the heroic age of aviation – the age of the first non-stop crossing of the Atlantic, by Alcock and Brown (p.42), Lindbergh's brave solo crossing (p.26) and Kingsford Smith's epic flight over the Pacific in 1928. Feats like these inspired confidence in aviation and, for the first time, planes began to carry passengers regularly. All over the world, new airlines went into business, and more and more people experienced the speed and novelty of flying. Nowhere did air travel grow more than in the USA, where mail contracts helped finance the emerging airlines. Here, especially, passenger aircraft design made rapid progress and, in 1933, Boeing launched the 247, the world's first modern airliner.

STARS IN THE SKY
Air travel was a new and glamorous experience, and many of the first passengers on the prestigious London-Paris route were American film stars or sports celebrities.

Metal skin of the plane made strong enough ("stressed") for bracing wires and struts to be unnecessary

THIS IS YOUR CAPTAIN
When the Instone shipping line launched an airline in 1919, their pilots wore the blue uniforms of a ship's captain. This is now standard dress for airline pilots.

CROYDON AIRPORT
Early airports were often little more than a grass landing strip and a straggle of tents. The world's first modern airport was built at Croydon near London in 1928.

Flight deck with automatic pilot to reduce stress on the pilot during long flights – a very advanced feature for the 1930s

Pressure tube for airspeed indicator

BOEING 247D
The Boeing 247D was one of the most advanced planes of its time. It had smooth monoplane wings, a streamlined, all-metal "skin", and an undercarriage that retracted into the wing in flight. All this helped cut aerodynamic drag so much that the 247D could fly at almost 300 kmh (180 mph) – faster than most fighter planes. Passengers could be whisked right across the USA in under 20 hours.

Front view of Boeing 247D

Boeing 247D in flight with undercarriage retracted

De Havilland Dragon

HARDY TRAVELLERS
Early passenger planes were tiny in comparison to those of today. The De Havilland Dragon of 1933 (above and right) was one of the smallest, carrying only eight passengers. But even the big Boeing 247D took only ten. Fixed rows of seats only became standard in the 1930s; the first passengers rode in loose wicker armchairs. Even in the 1930s, a long plane journey could be quite an ordeal. Without the pressurized cabins of today (pp. 34-35), airliners tended to fly low and passengers were shaken about all over the place by turbulence. If they flew high to avoid the weather, the poor passengers might endure bitter cold and altitude sickness.

Passenger cabin of De Havilland Dragon

Highly reliable 550 hp Pratt and Whitney "Wasp" air-cooled radial engine

Variable pitch propellers (p. 31) to give both high cruising speed and extra power for take-off

Tailplane

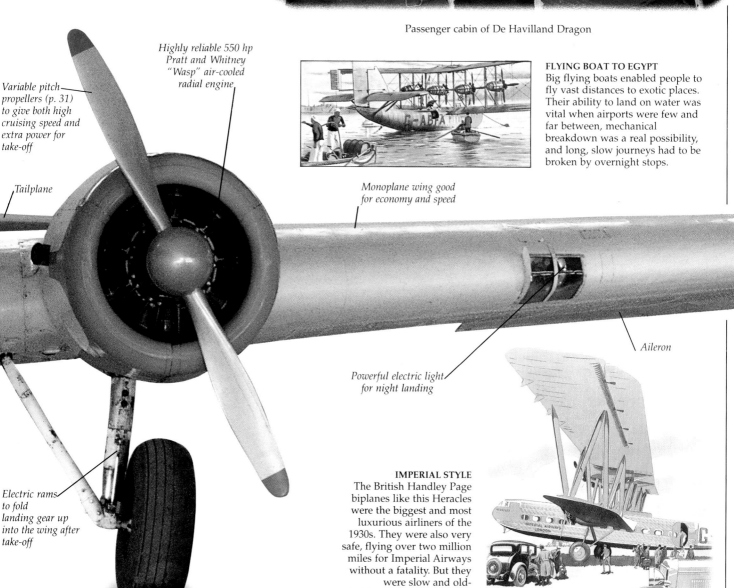

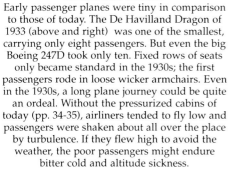

FLYING BOAT TO EGYPT
Big flying boats enabled people to fly vast distances to exotic places. Their ability to land on water was vital when airports were few and far between, mechanical breakdown was a real possibility, and long, slow journeys had to be broken by overnight stops.

Monoplane wing good for economy and speed

Aileron

Powerful electric light for night landing

Electric rams to fold landing gear up into the wing after take-off

IMPERIAL STYLE
The British Handley Page biplanes like this Heracles were the biggest and most luxurious airliners of the 1930s. They were also very safe, flying over two million miles for Imperial Airways without a fatality. But they were slow and old-fashioned compared to the American airliners.

33

Jetliner

THE JET AIRLINER has transformed air travel since the 1950s. Before then, only the wealthy could afford to fly. Now millions of ordinary people travel by air each year. Jetliners are not only fast and quiet compared to earlier planes. They can also fly high above the weather, carrying passengers smoothly in cabins "pressurized" to protect them from the reduction in air pressure at this height. In outline, the jets of today look little different from those of 30 years ago, but beneath the skin, there is a great deal of advanced technology. Sophisticated electronic control and navigation systems have made jetliners much safer to fly in. Airframes now include light, strong carbon-fibre and other "composite" materials. Computer-designed wings cut fuel costs. And advanced turbofan engines keep engine noise to a minimum.

ARMCHAIRS IN THE SKY
The smoothness of the engines, low cabin noise, and high-altitude flying made jetliners very comfortable.

BIT BY BIT
Modern jetliners are built up in sections and bolted, rivetted, and bonded together with strong adhesive. To keep joints to a minimum, the sections are as few as possible.

FUSELAGE SECTION
The fuselage tube is the same diameter over most of its length. This makes it cheap and easy to construct, because all the frames and tube pieces are the same size and shape. And if the manufacturer wants to make the plane longer or shorter, all that has to be done is add or take away a fuselage section or "plug".

Mounting for wing root, containing central fuel tank

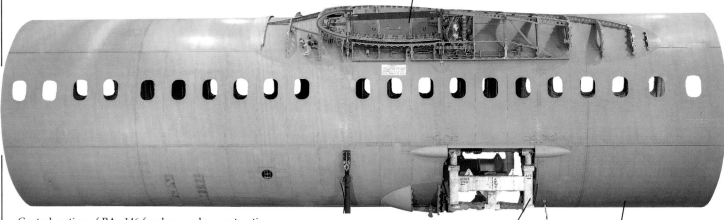

Central section of BAe 146 fuselage under construction

Jack placed in the undercarriage recess to support the fuselage during construction

Green chromate-based anti-corrosion treatment, prior to painting

Cavity for fuel tank

Wing skin made from a single piece of metal for extra strength

THE WING
As wing design has improved, so the wings of jetliners have become slimmer in comparison to the wings of older airliners (pp. 32-33). This keeps drag to a minimum. Because they cruise at high speeds, jetliner wings must also carry a complicated array of flaps and ailerons, for extra lift and control at low speeds for take-off and landing, and spoiler flaps (air brakes) to slow the plane down quickly after landing.

Engine mounting pylon

Mounting for inner flaps or spoilers that flip up to slow the plane down after landing

Hydraulic flap control pipe

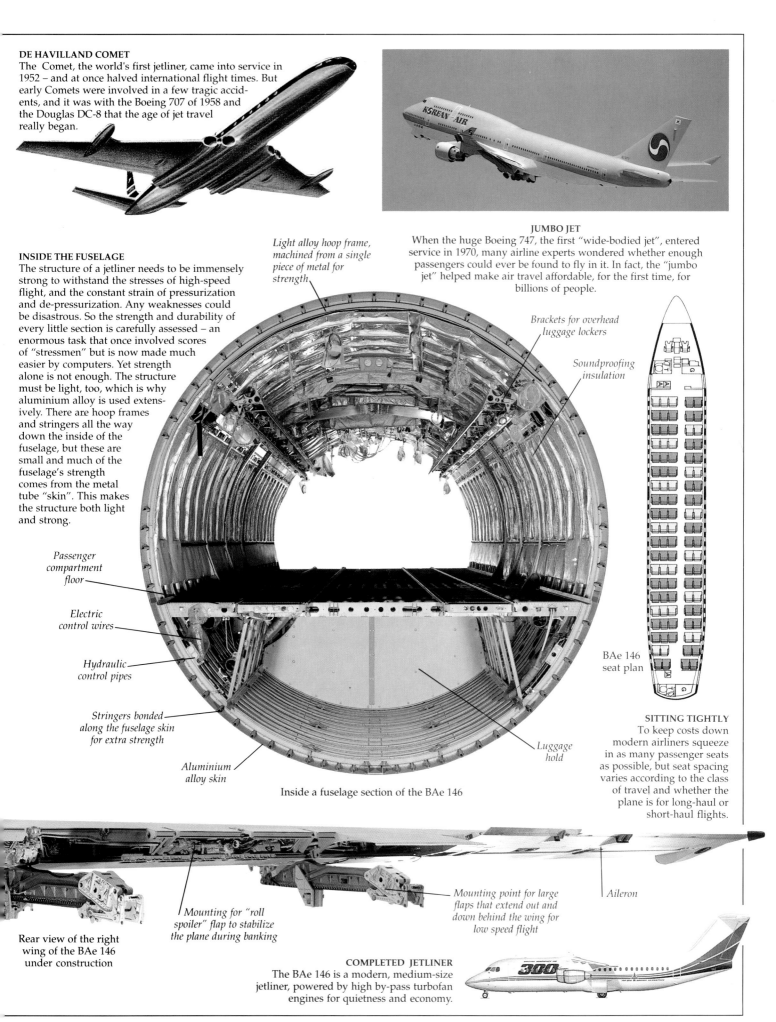

DE HAVILLAND COMET

The Comet, the world's first jetliner, came into service in 1952 – and at once halved international flight times. But early Comets were involved in a few tragic accidents, and it was with the Boeing 707 of 1958 and the Douglas DC-8 that the age of jet travel really began.

JUMBO JET

When the huge Boeing 747, the first "wide-bodied jet", entered service in 1970, many airline experts wondered whether enough passengers could ever be found to fly in it. In fact, the "jumbo jet" helped make air travel affordable, for the first time, for billions of people.

INSIDE THE FUSELAGE

The structure of a jetliner needs to be immensely strong to withstand the stresses of high-speed flight, and the constant strain of pressurization and de-pressurization. Any weaknesses could be disastrous. So the strength and durability of every little section is carefully assessed – an enormous task that once involved scores of "stressmen" but is now made much easier by computers. Yet strength alone is not enough. The structure must be light, too, which is why aluminium alloy is used extensively. There are hoop frames and stringers all the way down the inside of the fuselage, but these are small and much of the fuselage's strength comes from the metal tube "skin". This makes the structure both light and strong.

Light alloy hoop frame, machined from a single piece of metal for strength

Brackets for overhead luggage lockers

Soundproofing insulation

Passenger compartment floor

Electric control wires

Hydraulic control pipes

Stringers bonded along the fuselage skin for extra strength

Aluminium alloy skin

Luggage hold

BAe 146 seat plan

Inside a fuselage section of the BAe 146

SITTING TIGHTLY

To keep costs down modern airliners squeeze in as many passenger seats as possible, but seat spacing varies according to the class of travel and whether the plane is for long-haul or short-haul flights.

Rear view of the right wing of the BAe 146 under construction

Mounting for "roll spoiler" flap to stabilize the plane during banking

Mounting point for large flaps that extend out and down behind the wing for low speed flight

Aileron

COMPLETED JETLINER

The BAe 146 is a modern, medium-size jetliner, powered by high by-pass turbofan engines for quietness and economy.

Jet propulsion

THE BIRTH OF THE JET ENGINE in the late 1930s marked a revolution in aviation. Some very highly tuned piston-engined planes were then flying at speeds in excess of 700 kmh (440 mph) – but only by burning a great deal of fuel. Jet engines made speeds like this so easy to achieve that, by the early 1960s, even big airliners on scheduled services were flying faster – and some military jets could streak along at 2,500 kmh (1,500 mph), more than twice the speed of sound. Now, almost all airliners, most military planes, and many small business planes ("executive jets") are powered by one of the several different kinds of jet engine. With the exception of Concorde, supersonic flight has proved too noisy and expensive for airliners, but jet engine technology is still making steady progress.

PIONEER JET
The first prototype jet engines were built at the same time by Pabst von Ohain in Germany and Frank Whittle in Britain – although neither knew of the other's work. Whittle's engine was first used in the Gloster E28/39 of 1941 (above).

BREAKING THE SOUND BARRIER
In 1947, in the specially built Bell X-1 rocket plane, test pilot Chuck Yeager succeeded in flying faster than sound – about 1,100 kmh (700 mph).

Turbine power

Jet engines should really be called "gas turbines". Like piston engines, their power comes from burning fuel. The difference is that they burn fuel continuously to spin the blades of a turbine rather than intermittently to push on a piston. In a turbojet, the turbine simply turns the compressor. In a turbofan, it drives the big fan at the front as well.

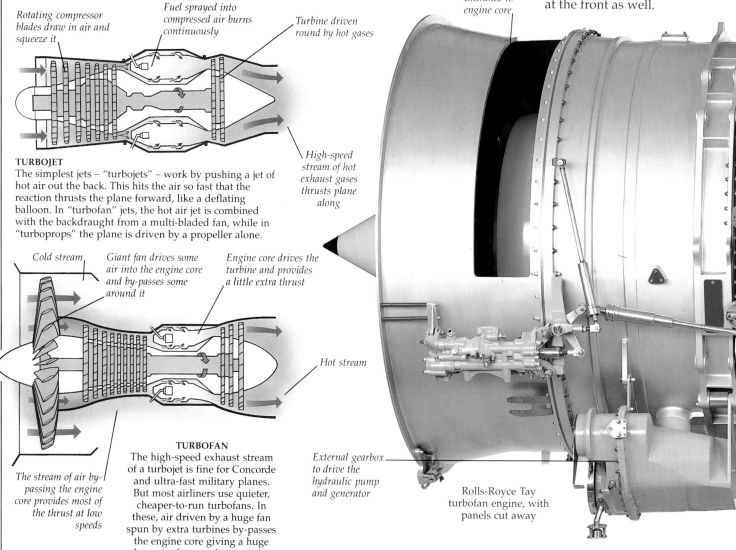

Rotating compressor blades draw in air and squeeze it

Fuel sprayed into compressed air burns continuously

Turbine driven round by hot gases

High-speed stream of hot exhaust gases thrusts plane along

TURBOJET
The simplest jets – "turbojets" – work by pushing a jet of hot air out the back. This hits the air so fast that the reaction thrusts the plane forward, like a deflating balloon. In "turbofan" jets, the hot air jet is combined with the backdraught from a multi-bladed fan, while in "turboprops" the plane is driven by a propeller alone.

Cold stream

Giant fan drives some air into the engine core and by-passes some around it

Engine core drives the turbine and provides a little extra thrust

Hot stream

The stream of air by-passing the engine core provides most of the thrust at low speeds

TURBOFAN
The high-speed exhaust stream of a turbojet is fine for Concorde and ultra-fast military planes. But most airliners use quieter, cheaper-to-run turbofans. In these, air driven by a huge fan spun by extra turbines by-passes the engine core giving a huge boost in thrust at low speeds.

Entrance to engine core

External gearbox to drive the hydraulic pump and generator

Rolls-Royce Tay turbofan engine, with panels cut away

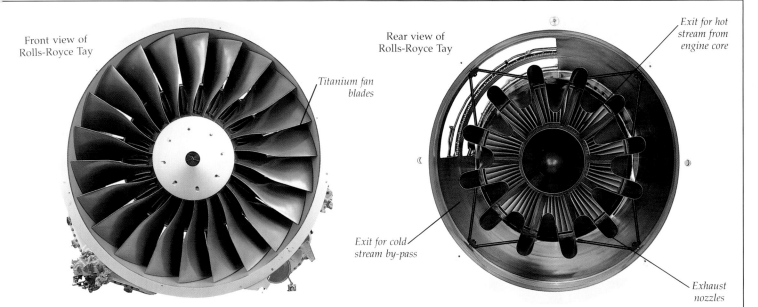

Front view of
Rolls-Royce Tay

Titanium fan blades

Rear view of
Rolls-Royce Tay

Exit for hot stream from engine core

Exit for cold stream by-pass

Exhaust nozzles

POWER FAN
Modern turbofan engines owe much of their immense power to the giant fan at the front, and the design of the fan blades has a critical effect on fuel economy. In the Rolls-Royce Tay, the fan pushes more than three times as much air through the by-pass duct to provide propulsion as through the engine core. In earlier turbofans, the proportions were about equal.

Combustion chamber where fuel spray burns continuously in the compressed air

BLOWING HOT AND COLD
Most of the turbofan's propulsive power is provided by the "cold-stream" air, rushing through the by-pass duct. The faster, "hot-stream" gas from the engine shoots out through the lobed exhaust nozzles. The lobes help mix the hot and cold streams quickly and reduce noise.

By-pass casing made of carbon fibre and plastic honeycomb for lightness and sound insulation

Turbines made of exotic metal alloys to endure running red hot all the time

BEYOND SOUND
The only successful supersonic airliner, Concorde flies the Atlantic twice as fast as conventional jets. But its turbojet engines can be noisy.

Rows of rotating compressor blades drive air through the engine, compressing the air as it passes through

Landing gear

THE FIRST AEROPLANES landed on wheels borrowed from motorcycles and cars, mounted on wooden or metal struts. They did the job, but the shock of a poor landing was often enough to make the struts collapse. Soon the "under-carriage" was given basic springs to cushion the blow and special aviation wheels were designed. But as planes grew heavier and landing and take-off speeds rose, wooden struts and wire wheels gave way to pressed-steel wheels and strong fluid-damped landing legs. Wheels were also mounted further apart on the wings for extra stability. From the 1940s on, wheels on all but the smallest, slowest planes were folded up into the wings in flight to cut down air resistance. With the coming of the jet age after World War II, the demands on landing gear increased still further. It was on jetliner landing gear that innovations later adopted on cars, such as disc and "anti-lock" brakes, were first tried. Modern jetliner undercarriages are highly sophisticated pieces of machinery with elaborate suspension and braking systems – designed to support the full force of a 150-tonne plane landing at 200 kmh (125 mph) or more and bring it quickly and safely to a halt.

LANDING ON WATER
In the days when good landing strips were few and far between, it made sense to land on water. On seaplanes, a step, two-thirds along the underside of the float, helped it "plane" on the water like a speed boat. This cut water drag enough for the aircraft to reach take-off speed.

LIGHTLY SPOKED
There were no brakes on this wheel from a pre-World War I plane. So it did not need elaborate criss-crossed spokes to resist braking forces.

Wooden landing strut

Skids to keep the plane from tipping forward when landing on soft ground

Elasticated rubber shock absorbers

SPRUNG TAIL-SKID
The rear ends of the pioneers' planes were so light, there was no need for a wheel; a simple skid was enough.

COMING DOWN GENTLY
The 1909 Deperdussin came down so lightly and slowly that elasticated rubber straps made fairly effective landing springs. Curved skids on the front helped to stop the plane pitching forward when landing on soft ground – a common hazard in the early days.

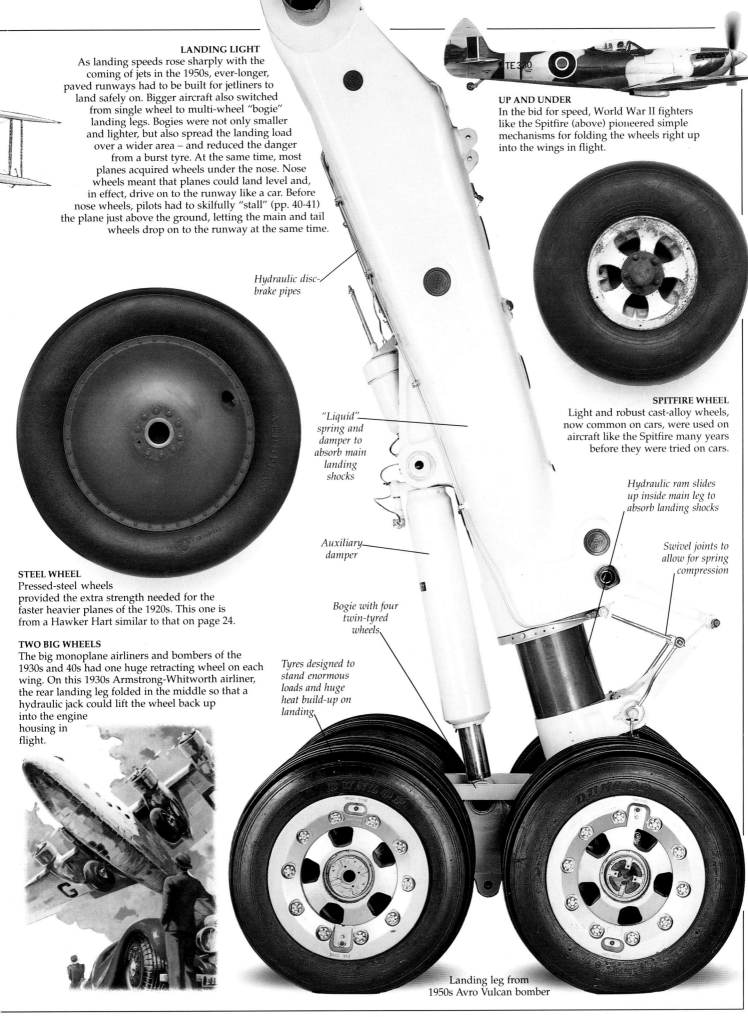

LANDING LIGHT

As landing speeds rose sharply with the coming of jets in the 1950s, ever-longer, paved runways had to be built for jetliners to land safely on. Bigger aircraft also switched from single wheel to multi-wheel "bogie" landing legs. Bogies were not only smaller and lighter, but also spread the landing load over a wider area – and reduced the danger from a burst tyre. At the same time, most planes acquired wheels under the nose. Nose wheels meant that planes could land level and, in effect, drive on to the runway like a car. Before nose wheels, pilots had to skilfully "stall" (pp. 40-41) the plane just above the ground, letting the main and tail wheels drop on to the runway at the same time.

UP AND UNDER

In the bid for speed, World War II fighters like the Spitfire (above) pioneered simple mechanisms for folding the wheels right up into the wings in flight.

Hydraulic disc-brake pipes

SPITFIRE WHEEL

Light and robust cast-alloy wheels, now common on cars, were used on aircraft like the Spitfire many years before they were tried on cars.

"Liquid" spring and damper to absorb main landing shocks

Hydraulic ram slides up inside main leg to absorb landing shocks

Swivel joints to allow for spring compression

Auxiliary damper

STEEL WHEEL

Pressed-steel wheels provided the extra strength needed for the faster heavier planes of the 1920s. This one is from a Hawker Hart similar to that on page 24.

TWO BIG WHEELS

The big monoplane airliners and bombers of the 1930s and 40s had one huge retracting wheel on each wing. On this 1930s Armstrong-Whitworth airliner, the rear landing leg folded in the middle so that a hydraulic jack could lift the wheel back up into the engine housing in flight.

Bogie with four twin-tyred wheels

Tyres designed to stand enormous loads and huge heat build-up on landing

Landing leg from 1950s Avro Vulcan bomber

Controlling the plane

A CAR OR A BOAT can only be steered to the left or right, but an aeroplane can be controlled in three dimensions. It can "pitch" nose-up or nose-down to climb or dive. It can "roll" from side to side, dipping one wing or the other. And it can "yaw" to the left or to the right, like a car steering. For many in-flight manoeuvres the pilot has to use not just one control, but all three simultaneously – which is why flying demands good co-ordination. Indeed, all the time the plane is in the air, the pilot must constantly trim the controls simply to keep the plane flying straight and level – for even on the calmest day, there is air turbulence to tip it off balance. "Automatic pilots" compensate for such upsets and make life for the pilot much easier.

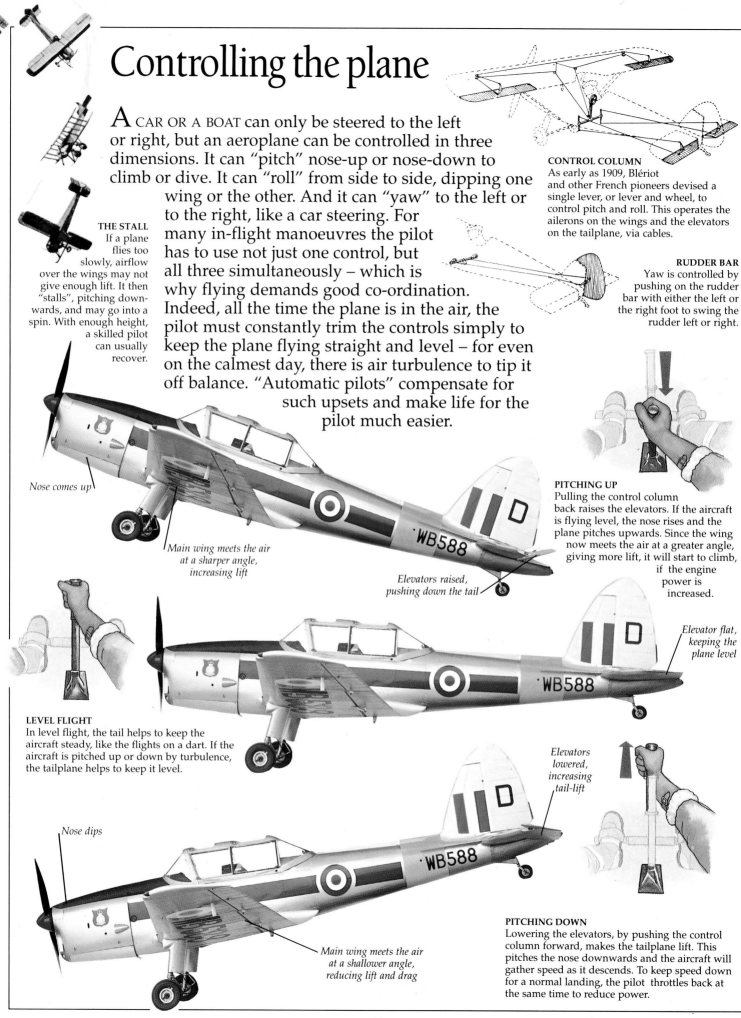

CONTROL COLUMN
As early as 1909, Blériot and other French pioneers devised a single lever, or lever and wheel, to control pitch and roll. This operates the ailerons on the wings and the elevators on the tailplane, via cables.

RUDDER BAR
Yaw is controlled by pushing on the rudder bar with either the left or the right foot to swing the rudder left or right.

THE STALL
If a plane flies too slowly, airflow over the wings may not give enough lift. It then "stalls", pitching downwards, and may go into a spin. With enough height, a skilled pilot can usually recover.

Nose comes up

Main wing meets the air at a sharper angle, increasing lift

Elevators raised, pushing down the tail

PITCHING UP
Pulling the control column back raises the elevators. If the aircraft is flying level, the nose rises and the plane pitches upwards. Since the wing now meets the air at a greater angle, giving more lift, it will start to climb, if the engine power is increased.

LEVEL FLIGHT
In level flight, the tail helps to keep the aircraft steady, like the flights on a dart. If the aircraft is pitched up or down by turbulence, the tailplane helps to keep it level.

Elevator flat, keeping the plane level

Nose dips

Elevators lowered, increasing tail-lift

Main wing meets the air at a shallower angle, reducing lift and drag

PITCHING DOWN
Lowering the elevators, by pushing the control column forward, makes the tailplane lift. This pitches the nose downwards and the aircraft will gather speed as it descends. To keep speed down for a normal landing, the pilot throttles back at the same time to reduce power.

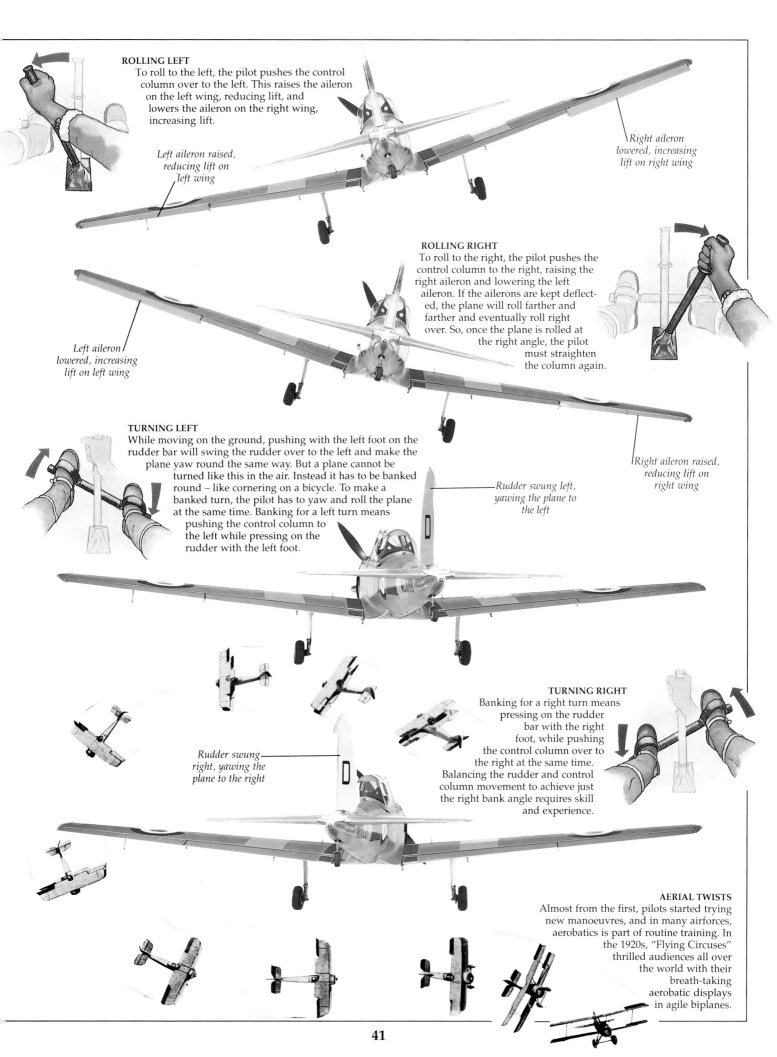

ROLLING LEFT

To roll to the left, the pilot pushes the control column over to the left. This raises the aileron on the left wing, reducing lift, and lowers the aileron on the right wing, increasing lift.

Left aileron raised, reducing lift on left wing

Right aileron lowered, increasing lift on right wing

ROLLING RIGHT

To roll to the right, the pilot pushes the control column to the right, raising the right aileron and lowering the left aileron. If the ailerons are kept deflected, the plane will roll farther and farther and eventually roll right over. So, once the plane is rolled at the right angle, the pilot must straighten the column again.

Left aileron lowered, increasing lift on left wing

Right aileron raised, reducing lift on right wing

TURNING LEFT

While moving on the ground, pushing with the left foot on the rudder bar will swing the rudder over to the left and make the plane yaw round the same way. But a plane cannot be turned like this in the air. Instead it has to be banked round – like cornering on a bicycle. To make a banked turn, the pilot has to yaw and roll the plane at the same time. Banking for a left turn means pushing the control column to the left while pressing on the rudder with the left foot.

Rudder swung left, yawing the plane to the left

TURNING RIGHT

Banking for a right turn means pressing on the rudder bar with the right foot, while pushing the control column over to the right at the same time. Balancing the rudder and control column movement to achieve just the right bank angle requires skill and experience.

Rudder swung right, yawing the plane to the right

AERIAL TWISTS

Almost from the first, pilots started trying new manoeuvres, and in many airforces, aerobatics is part of routine training. In the 1920s, "Flying Circuses" thrilled audiences all over the world with their breath-taking aerobatic displays in agile biplanes.

In the cockpit

CLOSED-IN COCKPITS had to await the development of safety glass in the late 1920s. Up until then, pilots sat in the open, exposed to howling winds, freezing cold, and damp – with nothing more to protect them than a tiny windscreen and warm clothes. Naturally, comfort was a low priority in these open cockpits, and they were very basic and functional in appearance. There were few instruments, and engine gauges were just as often on the engine itself as in the cockpit. The layout of the main flight controls became established fairly early on, with a rudder bar at the pilot's feet for turning, and a control column or "joystick" between the knees for diving, climbing and banking. Some early planes had a wheel rather than a joystick but it served the same purpose. This basic layout is still used in light planes today.

Control wheel pivoted backward and forward for diving and climbing just like a control stick

DEPERDUSSIN 1909
The cockpits of the earliest planes were very simple, for they had no instruments. With a large fuel tank obscuring the view ahead, the pilot had to constantly lean out of the cockpit to check height, and attitude.

VICKERS VIMY 1919
The Vimy was designed towards the end of World War I for long-range British bombing raids over industrial targets in Germany, and the cockpit was laid out accordingly, with two seats - one for the pilot and one for the observer. The pilot had to read engine speed and oil pressure from gauges mounted on the engines themselves.

Clock

Altimeter to show height

ATLANTIC FLIGHT *above*
The Vimy was the plane in which John Alcock and Arthur Brown made the first non-stop flight over the Atlantic on 14-15 June 1919, enduring 16 hours of freezing fog and drizzle in an open cockpit.

Hand-wound magneto to provide electric current for starting

Instrument light switches

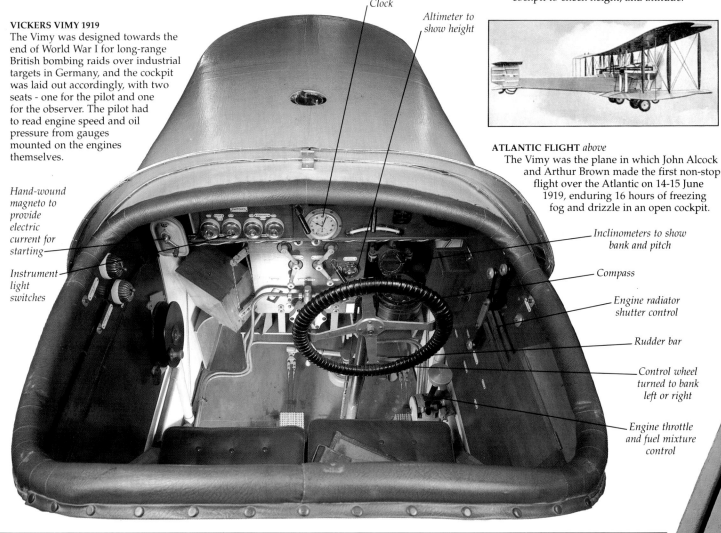

Inclinometers to show bank and pitch

Compass

Engine radiator shutter control

Rudder bar

Control wheel turned to bank left or right

Engine throttle and fuel mixture control

TIGER MOTH

By the 1930s, the "joystick" had become the standard form of control and even the simplest planes, like this De Havilland Tiger Moth, had a range of basic instruments: airspeed indicator, altimeter, turn indicator, compass, engine rev counter and oil pressure gauge. But there was still no artificial horizon to help the pilot keep the plane level, so the plane could only be flown in clear weather when the horizon was visible. The whole cockpit was functional and basic, with none of the comforts light planes usually have today, such as carpets, moulded seats, and heaters.

Turn indicator

Small windscreen

Notice saying "Aerobatic manoeuvres may be performed"

Engine rev counter

SKY TIGER

The DH Tiger Moth biplane was one of the most popular of all light planes in the 1930s. Simple and reliable, it was used for everything from training and crop-spraying to daring aerobatic displays.

Compass

Airspeed indicator

Altimeter

Joystick

Lever to close landing/take-off slats on the wing during aerobatic manoeuvres

Notice reminding the pilot that the plane can cruise at 150 kmh (94 mph) but will stall if the plane flies slower than 72 kmh (45 mph)

Engine oil pressure gauge

Rudder bar

Throttle

On the flight deck

THE FLIGHT DECK of a modern jetliner looks dauntingly complicated, with its array of switches, dials, and displays for such things as engine condition, hydraulics, navigational aid, and so on, not to mention the basic flight controls. Increasingly, however, computers are taking over certain functions, and the mass of dials is being replaced by neat screens called CRTs (for "cathode ray tube"), on which the pilot can change the information displayed at the flick of a button.

Landing and taxi light switches

Engine starting controls

Battery-powered, stand-by main flight instruments, enabling the pilot to land safely in case of complete electrical failure

Navigation computer equipment

Engine speed control (throttle)

Engine information such as fuel flow, turbine temperature, and torque

Indicators for brakes and hydraulic systems

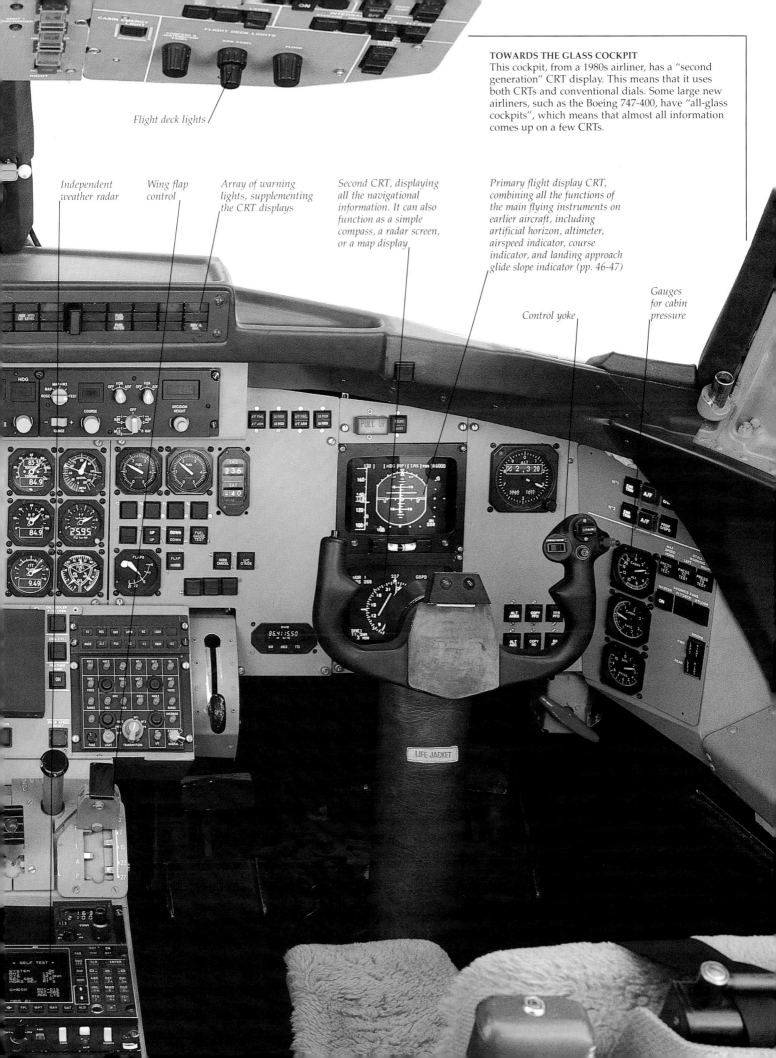

Flight deck lights

TOWARDS THE GLASS COCKPIT
This cockpit, from a 1980s airliner, has a "second generation" CRT display. This means that it uses both CRTs and conventional dials. Some large new airliners, such as the Boeing 747-400, have "all-glass cockpits", which means that almost all information comes up on a few CRTs.

Independent weather radar

Wing flap control

Array of warning lights, supplementing the CRT displays

Second CRT, displaying all the navigational information. It can also function as a simple compass, a radar screen, or a map display

Primary flight display CRT, combining all the functions of the main flying instruments on earlier aircraft, including artificial horizon, altimeter, airspeed indicator, course indicator, and landing approach glide slope indicator (pp. 46-47)

Control yoke

Gauges for cabin pressure

LIFE JACKET

Flying instruments

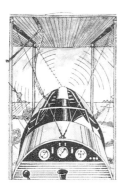

Pressure plate

Spring

T HE WRIGHT BROTHERS (p. 14) flew with nothing more in the way of instruments than an engine rev counter, a stopwatch, and a wind meter to tell them roughly how fast the plane was going. But the dangers of stalling (pp. 40-41) by flying too slow soon made it clear that every flying machine should have an accurate airspeed indicator as standard. As aircraft began to fly higher and further, an "altimeter" to indicate height and a magnetic compass to help keep a straight course were quickly added as well. Yet for a long time, pilots flew "by the seat of their pants", judging the plane's attitude by feel alone when they could not see. It was only with Elmer Sperry's development of gyroscope-stabilized instruments in 1929 that pilots were given a bank-and–turn indicator and an artificial horizon. Gyroscopes – a kind of spinning top that stays level no matter what angle the plane is at – enabled them to "fly on instruments" when visibility was poor.

DOUBLE TUBE
This is one of the first instruments to give a continuous and reliable indication of airspeed. It works by comparing "static" pressure (ordinary air pressure) to "dynamic" pressure (from the plane pushing forward). Its twin pipes point into the airflow, one running straight through but the other ending in a perforated cylinder. The pressure difference between the two, measured by a flexible diaphragm, indicates the airspeed.

Farnborough airspeed indicator c. 1909

Diaphragm

HOW FAST?
Among the earliest speed indicators were "anemometers" (wind meters) adapted from weather forecasting. The pilot got a rough idea of how fast the plane was going by timing so many seconds on a stopwatch while noting on the meter dials how many times the airflow turned the fan on the front.

Static pipe

Dynamic pipe

Static tube

Pitot head

Dynamic tube

PITOT HEAD
The twin-tube pressure method pioneered by Farnborough soon became the basis for measuring airspeed on all aircraft. The twin tube was refined into the pressure-sensing "pitot" head mounted on the airframe. Rubber tubes connected the pitot to the airspeed gauge in the cockpit.

Connecting tube

Gauge

Ogilvie airspeed indicator c. 1918

AIR SPEED

MACH METER
As jet planes approached and even exceeded the speed of sound in the 1950s, they were given "Mach meters". These showed how fast the plane was flying relative to the speed of sound.

MACH

SPEED LIMIT
In the years after World War II, airspeed indicators often had a pointer (arrow head) showing the maximum safe speed of the plane.

KNOTS

WING SPRING
This dates from 1910, but even in the 1930s some planes still used these simple devices. They showed airspeed according to how far the pressure plate was forced back against a spring by the airflow.

HOW STRAIGHT?
In this bank-and-turn indicator, a simple spirit level indicates how much the plane is banked. Changes in direction are shown by the upper turn needle, linked to an electrically driven gyroscope.

WHICH WAY?
Landing in poor weather was made much safer by this gyroscopic instrument. It helped the pilot maintain a course and glide slope set by a radio beam lined up with the runway.

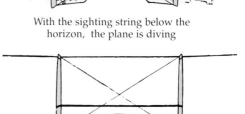

With the sighting string below the horizon, the plane is diving

With the sighting string above the horizon, the plane is climbing

HOW HIGH?
To tell how high they were, the pioneer aviators used to whip from their pockets little altimeters such as the Elliott (below) – similar to those used by mountaineers for years before. But the aerial antics of World War I fighters showed the need for a big dial fixed to the panel (left).

With the sighting string dipping left below the horizon, the plane is rolling left

HOW LEVEL?
In the early days, pilots could only look at the horizon, perhaps with the aid of a "sighting string" (above right), to tell them how much their machine was pitching or rolling. At night, or in thick cloud, the pilot would soon be completely disorientated. Research showed that even the most experienced pilot could not fly "blind" for more than eight minutes without getting into a spin. The answer was a gyroscopic artificial horizon

Inside the black box

All modern airliners and military planes now carry a "black box" or "Flight Data Recorder" to give a complete history of the flight in case of an accident. The box is connected up to all the aircraft's main systems and records everything that happens to it during the flight, monitoring flight deck instruments, engine data and even all that the crew says.

Connections to aircraft systems

Recorder motor

Kevlar lining to insulate the recorder against the heat of a fire

BOXED IN
All the data in this box is stored in eight tracks on a magnetic tape. An enormously strong, well insulated, titanium alloy case protects the tape against crash damage and fire.

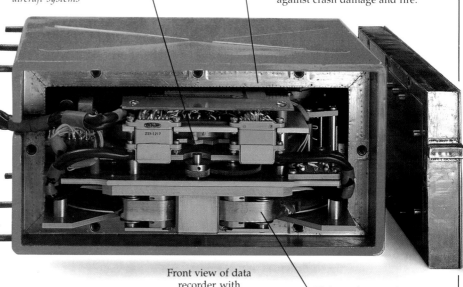

Front view of data recorder

Carrying handle

Front view of data recorder with cover removed

Eight-track magnetic tape for data recording

Rotating wings

The IDEA OF FLYING on rotating wings is old. As long ago as 1400, European children played with flying toys with whirring blades. Indeed, up until the Wright brothers' *Flyer*, many felt the future of flight lay with rotating rather than fixed wings. Spinning wings, they knew, would slice through the air to provide lift just like fixed wings (p. 11). But while a fixed wing plane must keep moving, a rotating wing plane could hover in one place. In the early 1900s, many whirling wing contraptions did lift some way off the ground. Yet the chances of controlled flight seemed remote until Juan de la Cierva created the "autogiro".

JUAN DE LA CIERVA
Cierva was obsessed from an early age with the idea of building a rotary-wing aircraft which he hoped would make flying safer.

Rotor blade

LOOK! NO WINGS
The autogiro was never meant to be a helicopter, but a plane without wings – a plane that was much safer than fixed wing planes because it would not stall simply by flying too slow. Indeed, Cierva's first autogiros did have stubby wings to assist take-off (right). Publicity for the autogiro always emphasized how it could drift safely to the ground, "slower than a parachute", in case of engine failure.

Autogiro

In early helicopter experiments, inventors had used ever more powerful engines to get their machines to rise. Cierva's stroke of genius was to see that rotating wings can provide lift without the engine. Like a sycamore pod whirling gently down to Earth, a freely rotating wing continues to spin by itself when moving through the air, pushed round by the pressure of air on the underside of the wings. He called this "self-rotation" or "autogiro".

CIERVA C-30
The C-30 was the most successful of all autogiros made in the 1930s. This example was one of many sold to the military for reconnaissance and acting as markers to set up radars in World War II.

Unique upswept tailplane with normal camber on this side only to counter-balance the rotation of the blades

Fabric-covered tube-steel fuselage similar to that of a biplane

Steerable tail-wheel

CARS OF THE SKY
For a while in the 1930s, many believed that autogiros would be the Model T Fords of the air – aircraft for everyone which would do away with traffic jams once and for all. Ads for the Pitcairn company, which made autogiros in the USA, were aimed clearly at the fashionable set. What could be simpler, they suggested, than to jump into the autogiro on your front lawn and drop in at your country club for a quick game of golf?

PIVOTING BLADES
Primitive rotor craft tended to roll over because the advancing blade cut through the air faster than the receding one, and so was lifted more. Cierva solved this problem with hinges that allowed the advancing blade to rise without affecting the plane.

Blade "lift" hinges

Sideways "drag" hinges and dampers allowing the blades to advance or trail slightly as they rotate to reduce the stress on the root of the blade

Hanging control column to allow the pilot to tilt the blades in any direction

Drive from the engine to start the rotors spinning for take-off

Rotor blade construction, showing how similar the profile is to conventional wings

SNAIL'S FLIGHT
To demonstrate its safety potential, the C-30 used to fly into the wind so slowly it could be outpaced by a runner.

150 hp Armstrong Siddeley seven-cylinder radial engine

Conventional propeller to pull the aircraft forward for take-off and normal flight

Soft oil-filled dampers to absorb landing shocks

Helicopter

SPINNING DREAMS
Helicopters have a long history, but many early experimenters were regarded as nutcases. Perhaps some of them were.

Of ALL FLYING MACHINES, none is quite so versatile as the helicopter. Its whirling rotor blades enable it to shoot straight up in the air, hover for minute after minute over the same spot, and land on an area little bigger than a bus. It burns up fuel at a frightening rate because the engine, via the rotors, provides all the lifting force. It also takes great skill to fly, for the pilot has three flight controls to handle - rudder, "collective pitch", and "cyclic pitch" controls - one more than conventional aircraft (pp. 40-41). But it has proved its worth in many situations, from traffic monitoring to dramatic rescues from sinking ships.

How a helicopter flies

A helicopter's rotor blades are really long, thin wings. The engine spins them round so that they cut through the air just like a conventional wing (p. 11). In a way, the rotor is also like a huge propeller, hauling the helicopter upwards just like the propeller pulls a plane along (p. 30).

THE TAIL-ROTOR
Without a tail-rotor, a helicopter would spin round in the opposite way to the rotor blades. The tail-rotor acts like a propeller to resist this "torque reaction". It is also a kind of rudder, and the pilot changes the pitch on its blades to swing the tail to the left or right.

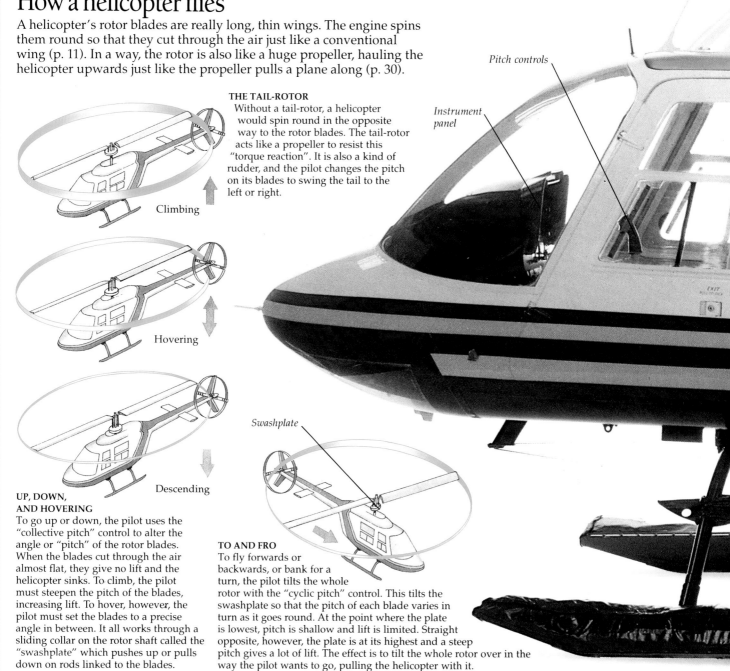

Pitch controls

Instrument panel

Climbing

Hovering

Descending

Swashplate

UP, DOWN, AND HOVERING
To go up or down, the pilot uses the "collective pitch" control to alter the angle or "pitch" of the rotor blades. When the blades cut through the air almost flat, they give no lift and the helicopter sinks. To climb, the pilot must steepen the pitch of the blades, increasing lift. To hover, however, the pilot must set the blades to a precise angle in between. It all works through a sliding collar on the rotor shaft called the "swashplate" which pushes up or pulls down on rods linked to the blades.

TO AND FRO
To fly forwards or backwards, or bank for a turn, the pilot tilts the whole rotor with the "cyclic pitch" control. This tilts the swashplate so that the pitch of each blade varies in turn as it goes round. At the point where the plate is lowest, pitch is shallow and lift is limited. Straight opposite, however, the plate is at its highest and a steep pitch gives a lot of lift. The effect is to tilt the whole rotor over in the way the pilot wants to go, pulling the helicopter with it.

Drag hinges flex to cut the strain on the rotor blades

Swivel for changing the rotor blade pitch

Rotor shaft

Link from swashplate (hidden) to adjust the pitch of the rotor blades in flight

BELL JETRANGER

The Bell JetRanger is one of a range of small, fast, all-purpose helicopters that appeared after the development of the gas turbine jet engines in the 1950s and 60s (pp. 36-37). In the days when they used piston engines, helicopters were rather specialized craft. The smoothness and reliability of jet engines, especially when running at near full power, made all the difference. Helicopters like the JetRanger, which can carry five people at speeds of up to 210 kmh (130 mph), are now used for an enormous range of everyday tasks from crop-spraying to short business trips.

400 hp Allison turboshaft jet engine

AERΩMEGA
HELICOPTERS

Landing skids

51

Continued on next page

CLIPPER OF THE CLOUDS

The idea of rotary-wing flight fired the imagination of many creative minds in the 19th century. The flying helicopter toys of Sir George Cayley (p. 10) were famous, but many other people built working models. These models did little more than climb up erratically into the air then drop. But the visionary inventor Gabriel de la Landelle was convinced that one day machines like the "Steam Airliner" he drew in 1863 (left) would sail majestically through the sky.

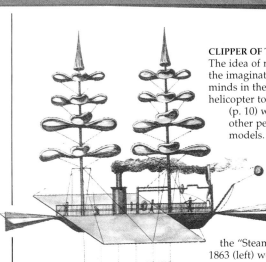

THE FIRST HELICOPTER FLIGHT?

Even in the early 20th century, many believed helicopters might still beat fixed wing planes into the air. They were wrong. Yet in 1907, just four years after the Wright brothers' first flight, this primitive tandem-rotor helicopter, built by French mechanic Paul Cornu, lifted him clear of the ground, if only for 20 seconds.

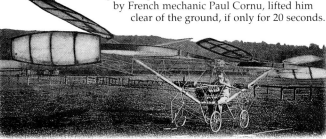

G-HUMT

Boom

Stabilizers to prevent boom from swinging up or down

Swashplate

Rotor blade pitch control rods

Leading edge of rotor blade

Pilot's seat

Engine housing

THE BIRTH OF THE HELICOPTER

Despite the early success of pioneers like Cornu, it proved immensely difficult to build a stable, controllable helicopter. The breakthrough only came with the invention of the autogiro (pp. 48-49) which taught how control could be achieved by altering the "pitch" (angle) of the rotor blades. In 1937, the German designer Heinrich Focke built a craft with an aeroplane fuselage and two huge rotors instead of wings. It could fly up and down, backwards and forwards, and even hover. Within months, another German, Anton Flettner, had built the first true helicopter – a nimble machine with two big blades that meshed like a cake whisk. Focke and Flettner used two rotors (turning in opposite directions) to prevent torque reaction (p. 50). But in 1939, Igor Sikorsky came up with the much simpler tail-rotor, and in his experimental VS-300 (above) pioneered the layout that has been used for helicopters ever since.

Gearbox

BUTTERFLY WINGS

The rubber-band-powered helicopter toys made by Alphonse Penaud and Dandrieux in the 1870s were the inspiration for many rotary wing enthusiasts.

HEAD IN A WHIRL

Once the practicality of the helicopter was proved in the late 1930s, people saw the possibilities for miniature, personal flying machines – including this bizarre back-pack designed by Frenchman George Sablier. It is not known whether it ever flew.

Tail fin

Tail rotor

HIGH TAIL

The tail-rotor resists the tendency for the helicopter to spin round in reaction to the rotor blades and acts as a rudder (p. 50). On this Bell helicopter, the main rotor blades turn clockwise (looking from above). So, to keep it straight, the tail-rotor must push the tail clockwise (towards you). To steer it to the left, the pilot flattens the tail rotor blades so that they push weakly and allow the tail to swing anticlockwise (away from you). To steer to the right, the pilot angles the tail-rotor blades more sharply to pull the tail strongly clockwise (towards you).

SIKORSKI R-4 1945 *below*

Igor Sikorsky was already a well-known aeroplane designer when he emigrated from Russia to the USA in 1917. As a teenager he had made many experiments with helicopters too, and in America in the 1930s he took them up again. After his success with the VS-300 in 1939, he quickly refined his design in a machine called the XR-4 – the "X" is for experimental. The US army were so sure of its merits that in 1942 they placed a large order for the new helicopter. The R-4 shown below is one of more than 400 built by the end of World War II.

Tail-rotor pitch control wires

Boom

KK995

AFGHANISTAN
The helicopter's ability to reach inaccessible places is invaluable in war.

Rear landing wheel

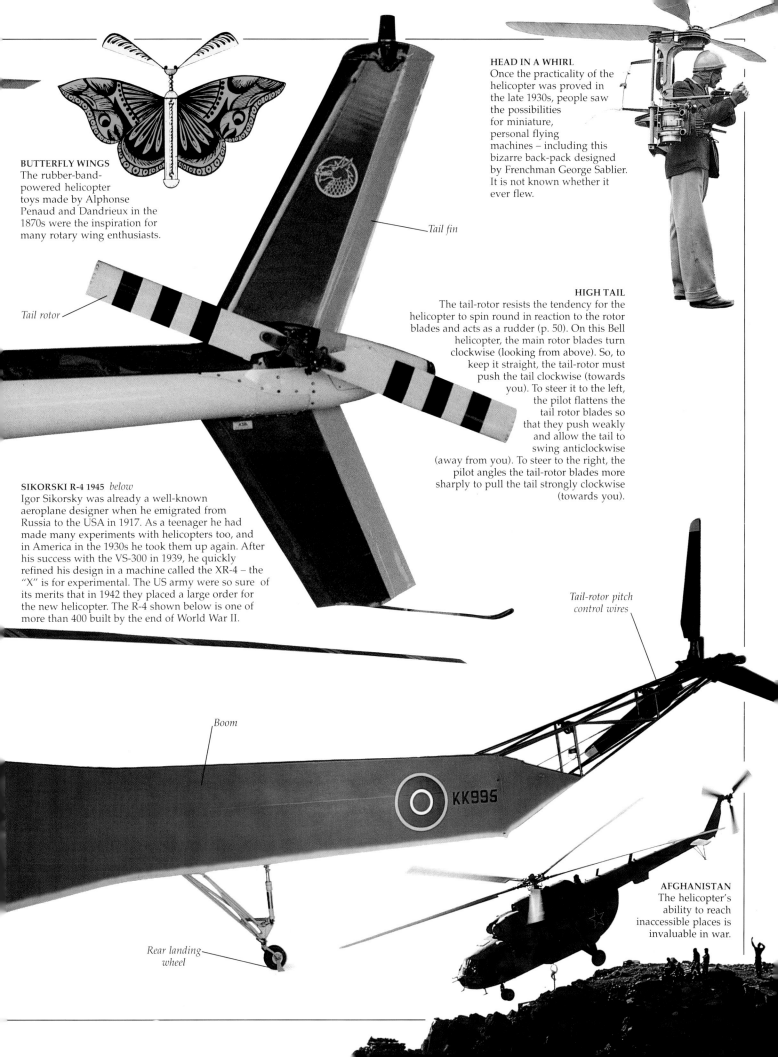

Hot-air balloon

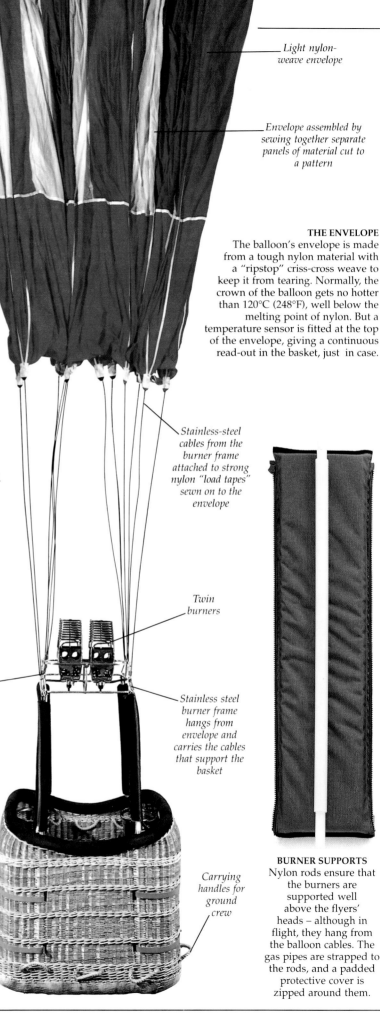

As a sport, ballooning all but died out after World War I – mainly because the gas to fill them had become too difficult and expensive to obtain. Then in the 1960s, Ed Yost, Tracy Barnes and others in the USA started to experiment with balloons inflated with hot air, just like the Montgolfier brothers' balloon nearly 200 years earlier. What was new about their balloons was that the envelopes were made of polyurethane-coated nylon, and they were filled by burning liquid propane gas. So successful was the combination that it sparked off a remarkable revival of interest in hot-air ballooning. Today, there are regular hot-air balloon events all over the world, as well as many attempts to break long-distance records.

Light nylon-weave envelope

Envelope assembled by sewing together separate panels of material cut to a pattern

THE ENVELOPE
The balloon's envelope is made from a tough nylon material with a "ripstop" criss-cross weave to keep it from tearing. Normally, the crown of the balloon gets no hotter than 120°C (248°F), well below the melting point of nylon. But a temperature sensor is fitted at the top of the envelope, giving a continuous read-out in the basket, just in case.

Stainless-steel cables from the burner frame attached to strong nylon "load tapes" sewn on to the envelope

UNCLE SAM
With the hot-air balloon revival, modern materials allowed balloon-makers to break away from the traditional balloon shape. At first, they made simple shapes such as drink cans and bottles. Now you may see a complete French chateau or two-humped camels floating gently through the sky.

Cables end in quick-release spring clips for easy assembly and dismantling

Twin burners

Stainless steel burner frame hangs from envelope and carries the cables that support the basket

BURNER SUPPORTS
Nylon rods ensure that the burners are supported well above the flyers' heads – although in flight, they hang from the balloon cables. The gas pipes are strapped to the rods, and a padded protective cover is zipped around them.

Carrying handles for ground crew

INFLATION
Filling the balloon is perhaps the trickiest part of the entire balloon flight. Here the burner is being used to inflate the balloon on the ground.

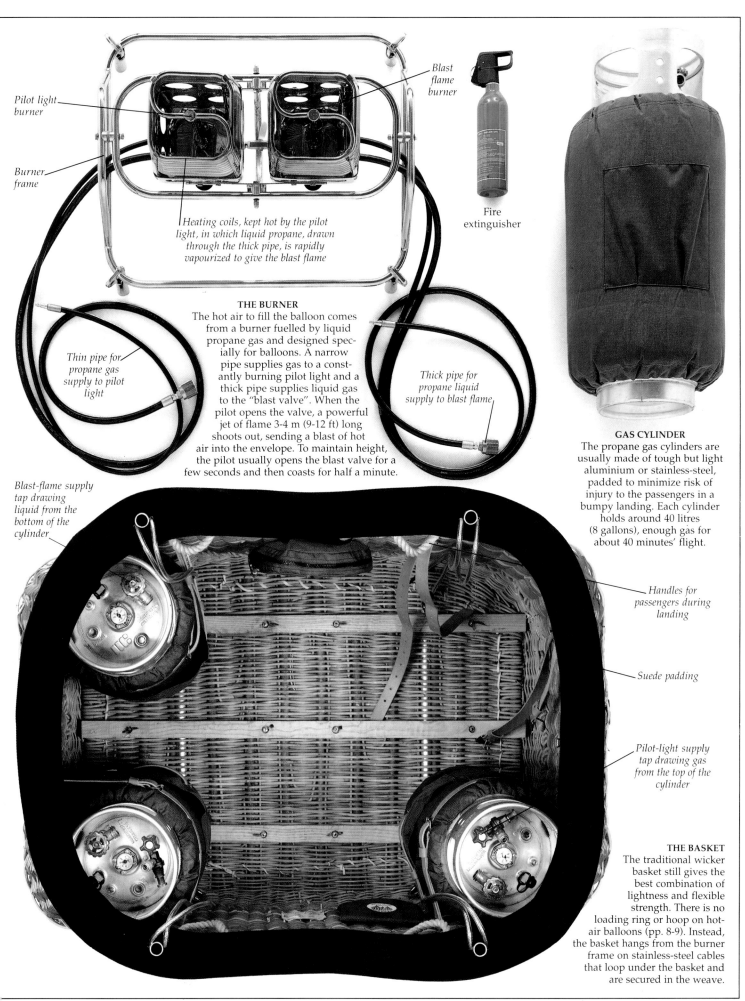

Pilot light burner

Burner frame

Blast flame burner

Heating coils, kept hot by the pilot light, in which liquid propane, drawn through the thick pipe, is rapidly vapourized to give the blast flame

Fire extinguisher

Thin pipe for propane gas supply to pilot light

THE BURNER
The hot air to fill the balloon comes from a burner fuelled by liquid propane gas and designed specially for balloons. A narrow pipe supplies gas to a constantly burning pilot light and a thick pipe supplies liquid gas to the "blast valve". When the pilot opens the valve, a powerful jet of flame 3-4 m (9-12 ft) long shoots out, sending a blast of hot air into the envelope. To maintain height, the pilot usually opens the blast valve for a few seconds and then coasts for half a minute.

Thick pipe for propane liquid supply to blast flame

GAS CYLINDER
The propane gas cylinders are usually made of tough but light aluminium or stainless-steel, padded to minimize risk of injury to the passengers in a bumpy landing. Each cylinder holds around 40 litres (8 gallons), enough gas for about 40 minutes' flight.

Blast-flame supply tap drawing liquid from the bottom of the cylinder

Handles for passengers during landing

Suede padding

Pilot-light supply tap drawing gas from the top of the cylinder

THE BASKET
The traditional wicker basket still gives the best combination of lightness and flexible strength. There is no loading ring or hoop on hot-air balloons (pp. 8-9). Instead, the basket hangs from the burner frame on stainless-steel cables that loop under the basket and are secured in the weave.

Airship

IT SEEMED THE DAYS OF AIRSHIPS WERE OVER when they were involved in a number of tragic accidents just before World War II (p. 9), and the giants of the inter-war years did indeed vanish. Yet the airship's ability to stay in the air for hour after hour was still useful for tasks like submarine surveillance. Right up until the late 1960s, small, non-rigid airships filled with safe, non-flammable helium gas were still being made. Then in the 1980s, Airship Industries began to produce a new generation of more substantial airships – made of modern materials, such as carbon-fibre and plastic composites, and filled with helium, not hydrogen, like the early airships.

UP IN FLAMES
Airships filled with hydrogen gas were always in danger from fire. Almost half the 72 airships flown by the German forces in World War I went up in flames, and the inferno that destroyed the *Hindenburg* (p. 9) signalled the end for the giant airships.

Strengthened glass-fibre nose cone to take mooring cable

SKYSHIP 500HL
Although big – about 55 m (170 ft) long – the Skyship 500HL is a fraction of the size of the pre-war giant airships, such as the *Hindenburg* which stretched 245 m (800 ft). However, there are plans to construct larger vessels, more than 120 m (400 ft) long. These will be able to stay in the air for a month or more at a time, to act as early warning stations for enemy attacks.

Automatic ballonet valve

Solid ballast for emergencies

Air scoops for filling ballonets

HANGING BASKET
Passengers and crew travel in a cabin beneath the envelope called the "gondola". Moulded from strong, lightweight carbon-fibre, it provides the same level of comfort as any modern aircraft. The flight deck, too, looks similar to that of a conventional plane – except there are no rudder pedals. In fact, since there are no ailerons (pp. 40-41), the pilot steers the airship by twisting the control column yoke to swing the rudder one way or the other.

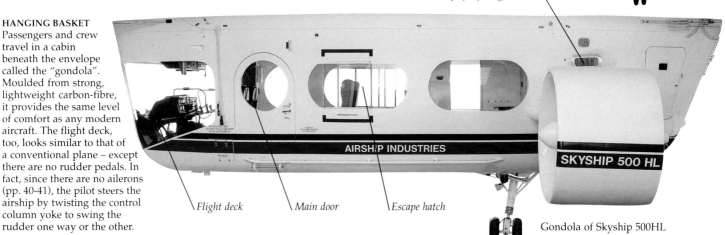

Flight deck

Main door

Escape hatch

AIRSHIP INDUSTRIES

SKYSHIP 500 HL

Gondola of Skyship 500HL

BLOW-OUT
When the airship rises, eight valves like this open automatically to let air out of the airbags.

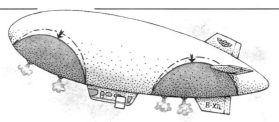

AIR BUBBLES
Inside the Skyship's helium-filled envelope are two air-filled bags called "ballonets", designed to reduce the loss of precious helium gas. As the airship climbs, atmospheric pressure drops and the gas expands. Rather than waste helium, automatic valves open to let air instead out of the ballonets (above). When the airship descends again, air is scooped in to refill the ballonets (right).

NOSE IN THE AIR
When climbing, the rear ballonet is kept fuller and heavier, helping the nose to come up. When descending, extra air is blown into the front ballonet, bringing the nose down.

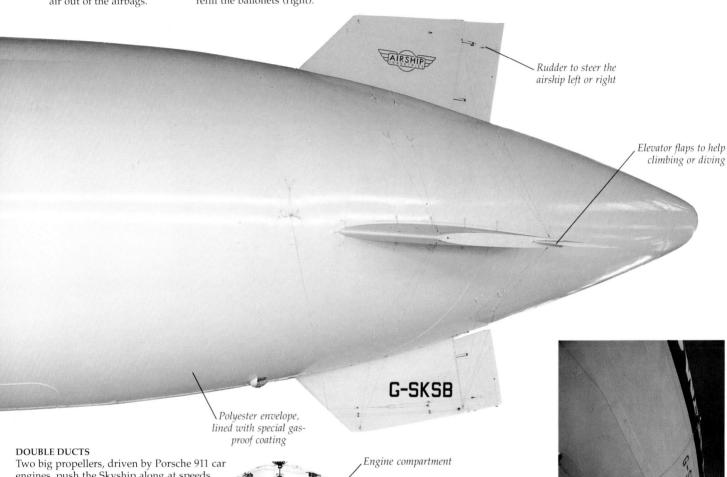

Rudder to steer the airship left or right

Elevator flaps to help climbing or diving

G-SKSB

Polyester envelope, lined with special gas-proof coating

DOUBLE DUCTS
Two big propellers, driven by Porsche 911 car engines, push the Skyship along at speeds of up to 160 kmh (100 mph). Each is enclosed in a duct to cut noise, increase propulsive efficiency, and protect groundstaff. Uniquely, both propellers swivel to "vector" (direct) thrust up or down for take-off and landing.

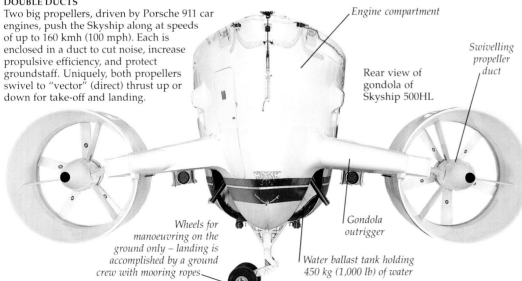

Engine compartment

Swivelling propeller duct

Rear view of gondola of Skyship 500HL

Wheels for manoeuvring on the ground only – landing is accomplished by a ground crew with mooring ropes

Gondola outrigger

Water ballast tank holding 450 kg (1,000 lb) of water

PUSHING UP AND DOWN
Swivelling propellers allow vertical take-offs. They also help the ship to land. Otherwise precious helium would have to be let out to make the ship heavier – especially when the fuel tank is empty and light after a long flight.

A modern glider

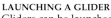

Although GLIDERS played a prominent part in the pioneering days of aviation (pp. 10-11), interest in them waned after powered flight was achieved. The problem was that, without power, gliders can only fly, in effect, "downhill" and, for a long time, no glider could stay up for more than a few seconds. Then, in the early 1920s, it was found that gliders could ride up on the wind rising over a ridge or hill, so that skilled pilots could stay aloft for hours at a time. A few years later, it was discovered that even away from hills, glider pilots could get a lift from "thermals" – bubbles of rising air warmed by the ground. Ever since, the sport of gliding has become more and more popular, and the glider has now evolved into one of the most aerodynamically efficient and elegant of all flying machines.

MASTER GLIDER
Birds of prey showed how to glide upwards on rising warm air.

LAUNCHING A GLIDER
Gliders can be launched in various ways. "Auto-towing" means using a powerful motor car to pull the glider along on a long cable until it climbs into the air. "Winch-launches" use a powerful winch in the same way. Both methods are cheap and quick, but will lift the glider no higher than 300 m (1,000 ft) or so. If the pilot cannot find lift from rising air quickly, the flight will last only a few minutes. An "aero-tow", using a powered plane to tug the glider into the air (below and right), is much more effective, but time-consuming and expensive.

Tug makes normal take-off with glider in tow

Powered "tug" plane tows glider on a 40 m (120 ft) tow rope

Airbrakes emerge from the wings at right-angles to steepen the descent for landing

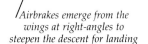

SLIPPERY SAILPLANE
Modern gliders such as this Schleicher K23 single-seater are made from GRP (glass reinforced plastic). This is not only strong and light, but can be moulded to give a super-smooth, low-drag surface. With such smooth lines and carefully profiled wings, a glider like this is very efficient aerodynamically – with, typically, a "glide ratio" of better than 1:45. This means it will usually drop only 1 m (3 ft) for every 45 m (150 ft) it flies. Competition gliders perform even better.

Down-turned wingtips stop ailerons fouling the ground and reduce turbulence at the wingtip

— *Aileron*

Instrument panel

Tow rope attached here for winch-launch or auto-tow

BAND-AID
In the days when many gliding clubs were on hill-tops, a "bungee" launch was often enough. A team ran towards edge of the hill pulling the glider on an elasticated rope. As the glider "unstuck" from the ground, it catapulted into the air.

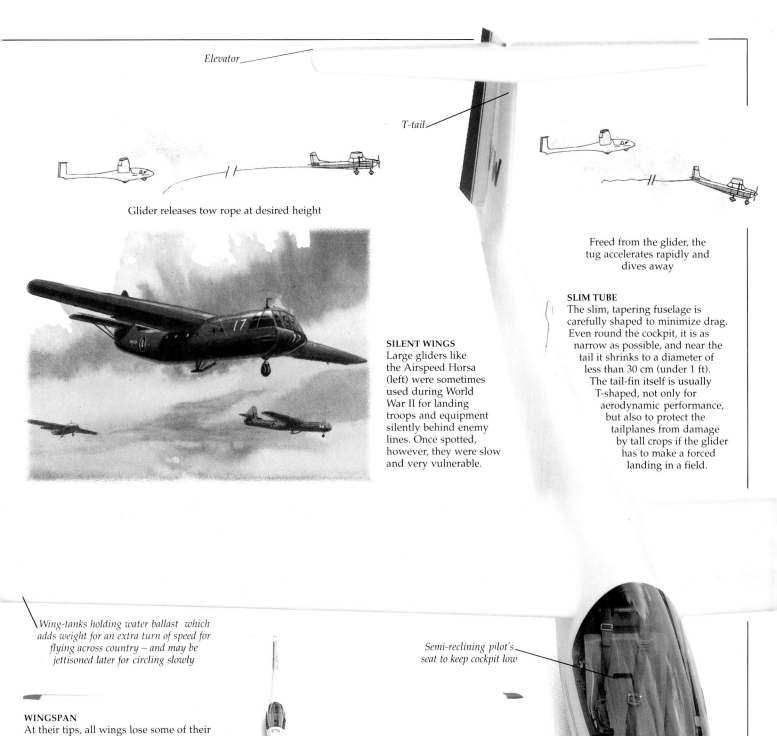

Elevator

T-tail

Glider releases tow rope at desired height

Freed from the glider, the tug accelerates rapidly and dives away

SLIM TUBE
The slim, tapering fuselage is carefully shaped to minimize drag. Even round the cockpit, it is as narrow as possible, and near the tail it shrinks to a diameter of less than 30 cm (under 1 ft). The tail-fin itself is usually T-shaped, not only for aerodynamic performance, but also to protect the tailplanes from damage by tall crops if the glider has to make a forced landing in a field.

SILENT WINGS
Large gliders like the Airspeed Horsa (left) were sometimes used during World War II for landing troops and equipment silently behind enemy lines. Once spotted, however, they were slow and very vulnerable.

Wing-tanks holding water ballast which adds weight for an extra turn of speed for flying across country – and may be jettisoned later for circling slowly

Semi-reclining pilot's seat to keep cockpit low

WINGSPAN
At their tips, all wings lose some of their lifting power because air flowing underneath curls over the top. The longer the wing is, the less important this effect is, so gliders have very long wings.

EVW

EVW

Rudder

Tow rope attached here for aero-tow

Kites for people

THE IDEA OF FLYING with a pair of wings alone seem to have been forgotten after the deaths of Lilienthal and other pioneer gliders around 1900 (pp.10-11). Then in the 1940s, an American called Francis Rogallo created a new kite plane using a fabric delta (triangular) wing. It was developed first simply as a steerable parachute for bringing equipment back to Earth from Space. But some people began to fly Rogallo wings by hanging beneath the wing and steering it by shifting weight. The idea caught on. Soon "hang-gliders" were running off hills all over the world. Hang-gliding is now one of the most popular aerial sports.

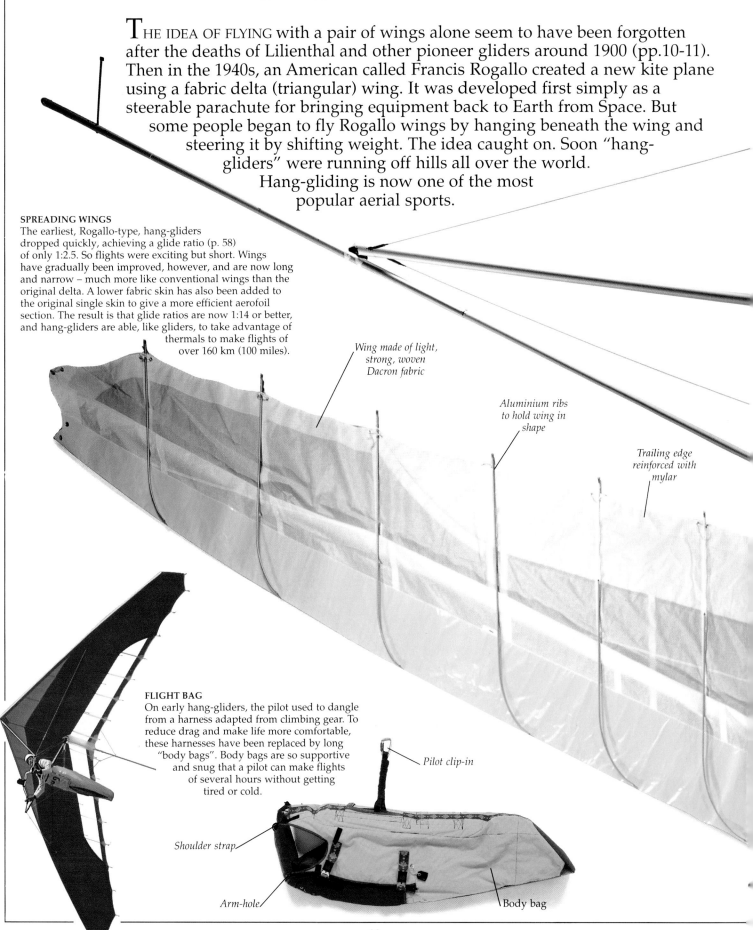

SPREADING WINGS
The earliest, Rogallo-type, hang-gliders dropped quickly, achieving a glide ratio (p. 58) of only 1:2.5. So flights were exciting but short. Wings have gradually been improved, however, and are now long and narrow – much more like conventional wings than the original delta. A lower fabric skin has also been added to the original single skin to give a more efficient aerofoil section. The result is that glide ratios are now 1:14 or better, and hang-gliders are able, like gliders, to take advantage of thermals to make flights of over 160 km (100 miles).

Wing made of light, strong, woven Dacron fabric

Aluminium ribs to hold wing in shape

Trailing edge reinforced with mylar

FLIGHT BAG
On early hang-gliders, the pilot used to dangle from a harness adapted from climbing gear. To reduce drag and make life more comfortable, these harnesses have been replaced by long "body bags". Body bags are so supportive and snug that a pilot can make flights of several hours without getting tired or cold.

Pilot clip-in

Shoulder strap

Arm-hole

Body bag

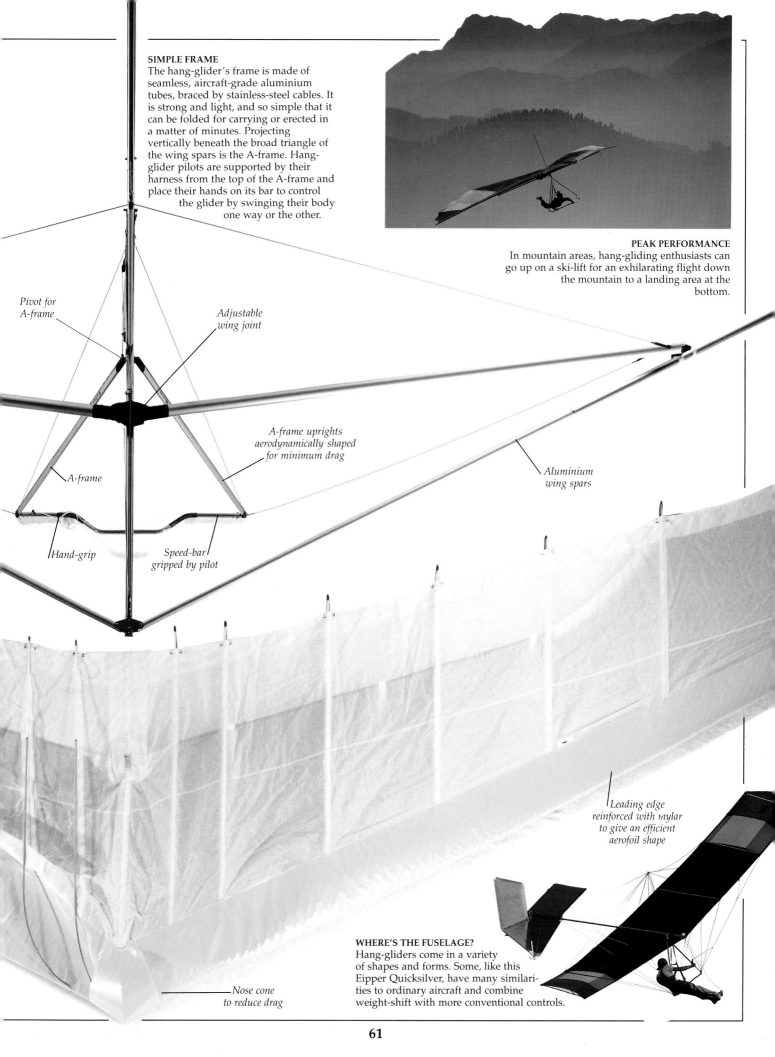

SIMPLE FRAME
The hang-glider's frame is made of seamless, aircraft-grade aluminium tubes, braced by stainless-steel cables. It is strong and light, and so simple that it can be folded for carrying or erected in a matter of minutes. Projecting vertically beneath the broad triangle of the wing spars is the A-frame. Hang-glider pilots are supported by their harness from the top of the A-frame and place their hands on its bar to control the glider by swinging their body one way or the other.

PEAK PERFORMANCE
In mountain areas, hang-gliding enthusiasts can go up on a ski-lift for an exhilarating flight down the mountain to a landing area at the bottom.

Pivot for A-frame

Adjustable wing joint

A-frame uprights aerodynamically shaped for minimum drag

Aluminium wing spars

A-frame

Hand-grip

Speed-bar gripped by pilot

Leading edge reinforced with mylar to give an efficient aerofoil shape

Nose cone to reduce drag

WHERE'S THE FUSELAGE?
Hang-gliders come in a variety of shapes and forms. Some, like this Eipper Quicksilver, have many similarities to ordinary aircraft and combine weight-shift with more conventional controls.

Portable planes

From the first days of powered flying, enthusiasts dreamed of a small aircraft, cheap enough and practical enough to be flown by ordinary people. Yet, until recently, even planes like the basic and popular De Havilland Moth series (p. 43) remained expensive, complicated machines. Then in 1973, Australian hang-glider pioneer Bill Bennett began experimenting with a hang-glider and a chainsaw motor driving a pusher propeller behind the pilot. It was not altogether safe, but it worked, and the "microlight" was born. Since then, the way the engine is fitted has became much more practical and safe, and the frame has been improved to take the extra load. Microlights are now flown all over the world. Some retain flexible wings (flex-wing) like hang-gliders. Others, especially in the USA and Australia (where they are known as "ultralights"), have developed into miniature aircraft with fixed wings and control surfaces.

Aluminium wing spar

Tensioning cable

THE FIRST MICROLIGHT?
Brazilian pioneer Alberto Santos-Dumont's tiny No. 19 monoplane had a wingspan of just 6 m (18 ft) and was perhaps the first microlight. He designed it in Paris in 1907 as an aerial "runabout" and could de-rig it to carry it on his car.

WIDE WING
Like the hang-glider on pages 60-61, a flex-wing microlight like this Solar Wings Pegasus Q has a shallow triangular wing of Dacron. But it is made broader than the hang-glider to lift the extra weight of the engine, trike, and two crew members.

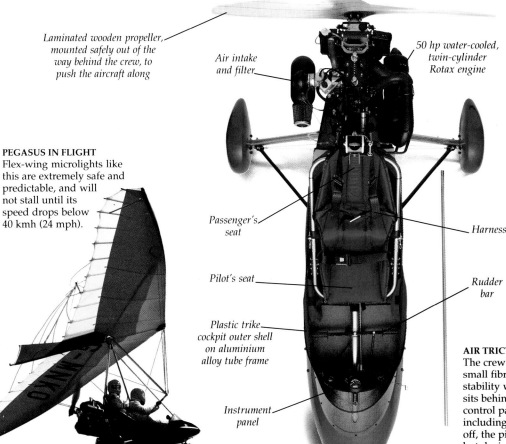

Laminated wooden propeller, mounted safely out of the way behind the crew, to push the aircraft along

Air intake and filter

50 hp water-cooled, twin-cylinder Rotax engine

PEGASUS IN FLIGHT
Flex-wing microlights like this are extremely safe and predictable, and will not stall until its speed drops below 40 kmh (24 mph).

Passenger's seat

Harness

Pilot's seat

Rudder bar

Plastic trike cockpit outer shell on aluminium alloy tube frame

Instrument panel

AIR TRICYCLE
The crew of a flex-wing microlight usually sit inside a small fibreglass car or "trike" with three-wheels for stability when landing and taking off. The passenger sits behind and slightly above the pilot, who faces a control panel with a small range of instruments including airspeed indicator and altimeter. For take-off, the pilot revs up the engine with the foot-throttle, but during flight, a steady cruise speed can be set with the hand-throttle. The Solar Wings Pegasus Q can climb at over 270 m (900 ft) a minute and cruises at 144 kmh (90 mph).

Streamlined nose cone

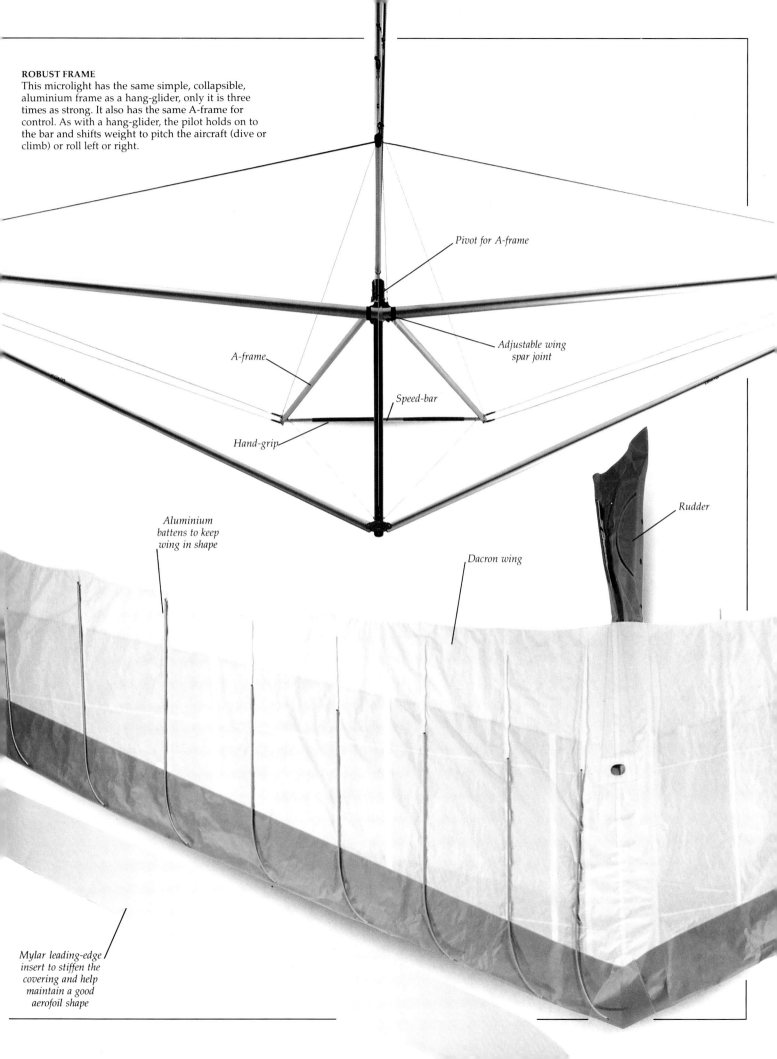

ROBUST FRAME
This microlight has the same simple, collapsible, aluminium frame as a hang-glider, only it is three times as strong. It also has the same A-frame for control. As with a hang-glider, the pilot holds on to the bar and shifts weight to pitch the aircraft (dive or climb) or roll left or right.

Pivot for A-frame

Adjustable wing spar joint

A-frame

Speed-bar

Hand-grip

Aluminium battens to keep wing in shape

Dacron wing

Rudder

Mylar leading-edge insert to stiffen the covering and help maintain a good aerofoil shape

Index

Acknowledgments

Dorling Kindersley would like to thank:
Aeromega Helicopters, Stapleford, England: pp. 50-51, 52-53
Airship Industries, London: pp. 56-57; and especially Paul Davie and Sam Ellery
Bristol Old Vic Theatre, Bristol, England, for studio space: pp. 54-55, 60-61, 62-63; and especially Stephen Rebbeck
British Aerospace, Hatfield: pp. 34-35, 44-45
Cameron Balloons, Bristol, England: pp. 54-55; and especially Alan Noble
Musée des Ballons, Forbes' Chateau de Balleroy, Calvados, France: pp. 8-9

Noble Hardman Aviation, Crickhowell, Wales: pp. 26-27
Penny and Giles, Christchurch, England: p. 47 (flight data recorder)
RAF Museum, Hendon, London: pp. 16-17, 23, 24, 29, 38-39, 48-49, 52-53; and especially Mike Tagg
SkySport Engineering, Sandy, Bedford, England: pp. 18-19, 20-21; and especially Tim Moore and all the team at SkySport
Rolls-Royce, Derby, England, pp. 36-37
Solar Wings Limited, Marlborough, England: pp. 60-61, 62-63; and especially John Fack
The Hayward Gallery, London, and Tetra Associates: pp. 6-7
The London Gliding Club,

Dunstable, England: pp. 59-59; and especial thanks to Jack Butler
The Science Museum, London: pp. 10-11, 12-13, 25, 28-29, 30-31, 39, 40, 46-47; and especially Peter Fitzgerald
The Science Museum, Wroughton, England: pp. 32-33; and especially Arthur Horsman and Ross Sharp
The Shuttleworth Collection, Old Warden Aerodrome, Bedford, England: pp. 14-15, 22, 38, 40-41, 42-43; and especially Peter Symes

John Bagley of the Science Museum for his help with the text

Lester Cheeseman for his desktop publishing expertise

Picture credits

Airship Industries: 57br
Austin J. Brown: 27tr; 35tr; 36tr; 55cl
British Aerospace: 35br, cr
Harmon: 53br
Hulton Picture Library: 9tc, br; 48tl; 52 tr
Jerry Young: 55bl
Mary Evans Picture Library: 6tc, bl; 8bl; 11tr, br; 14lc; 15 rc; 20tl; 21br; 26tl; 32tl; 33br; 39br; 48lc; 52tl; 53tl; 56tl
Michael Holford: 10tc
Popperfoto: 39 tr; 53tr
Quadrant: 49bc
Retrograph Archive: 6lc
Robert Hunt Library: 18bl
Solar Wings: 60bl, 62bl
The Science Museum, London: 10bl; 12bc; 13br
Zefa: 37br; 60tr, br

Illustration by: Mick Loates, Peter Bull
Picture research by: Suzanne Williams